Loyalty a

Those Who LEAVE YOU

DAG HEWARD-MILLS

Parchment House

Unless otherwise stated, all Scripture quotations are taken from the King James Version of the Bible

THOSE WHO LEAVE YOU

First published 2011 by Parchment House
16th Printing 2019

77Find out more about Dag Heward-Mills at:
Healing Jesus Campaign
Write to: evangelist@daghewardmills.org
Website: www.daghewardmills.org
Facebook: Dag Heward-Mills
Twitter: @EvangelistDag

ISBN : 978-9988-8500-5-0

Contents

CHAPTER 1

Why God Allows People to Leave You

Fifteen Reasons Why God Allows People to Leave You

There are several reasons why the Lord will allow people to leave you and even hurt you.

1. **The Lord may allow people to leave you to correct a foundational mistake in your ministry.**

At the beginning of ministry, we are often filled with the fear of failure. This fear of failure causes us to grasp at any help that comes our way. In the process of reaching out for help, many ministers attach themselves to the wrong people.

Abraham was a good example of this. God had told him to separate himself from his family and to go on a long and mystical journey to an undefined promised land. Instead of separating himself from his family as God had told him, Abraham went along with some family members and notable amongst them was Lot.

> Now the Lord had said unto Abram, get thee out of thy country, and FROM THY KINDRED, and from thy father's house, unto a land that I will shew thee:
>
> Genesis 12:1

> And Abram went up out of Egypt, he, and his wife, and all that he had, AND LOT WITH HIM, into the south.
>
> Genesis 13:1

All the problems that Abraham had on his journey can be traced to the presence of Lot in his life. Notice the problems that Abraham had because he had Lot with him.

1. Abraham had problems of strife and confusion because of Lot. Abram had to eventually separate from his relatives because of Lot (Genesis 13:7-8).

2. Abraham fought a war he would never have fought because of Lot. Abraham had to rescue Lot from King Chedorlaomer (Genesis 14:1-16).

3. Abraham had to intercede specially because of Lot. Abraham had to save his nephew from the destruction coming upon Sodom and Gomorrah (Genesis 18:23-33).

This is what I call a foundational mistake of the ministry. It is a mistake you make at the beginning of your ministry, and it is usually made out of fear. These mistakes can cause the wrong person to be attached like an albatross to all that you do.

Sometimes people even marry the wrong person when they are entering into ministry. God may remove that wrong person you have married from the earth so that you will be free from the albatross around your neck. If God does not remove this person from your life you will have to do your entire ministry with the albatross around your neck.

Certain people who were part of my ministry at the very beginning are no longer a part of what I do. Perhaps, I took some of these people along with me because I was afraid that

I could not succeed without them. Their presence gave me the reassurance that I would succeed. God in His mercy caused some of them to leave me. Even though I really missed some of them, I recognized that God allowed them to leave because it was a mistake in the first place to carry them along into my new vision to build the church.

2. The Lord may allow people to leave you to humble you.

> And thou shalt remember all the way which the Lord thy God led thee these forty years in the wilderness, TO HUMBLE THEE, and to prove thee, to know what was in thine heart, whether thou wouldest keep his commandments, or no.
>
> Deuteronomy 8:2

It is a humbling experience to have people desert, abandon or resign from your organisation. Every departure leaves a sour taste in your mouth. Every time someone departs unceremoniously, he leaves behind a trail of unanswered questions. The uncertainty created by people who leave is unsettling and truly humbling.

After planting churches for many years, I was blessed to have hundreds of loyal pastors, sons and daughters. I was also blessed to have some of my own relatives as pastors in the church.

However, one day some of my relatives abandoned me in the ministry and did the exact opposite of what I had been teaching. It was a great embarrassment to me as my own family members became the focus of rebellion and disloyalty in the church. I now had to combat my own family. It occurred to me many times that I had been able to induce loyalty in so many people but I could not do that in my own family.

I felt that God was humbling me through this process. He wanted to show me that it is not by might nor by power nor by teachings nor principles but by His grace alone. Perhaps, you have had some people leaving you. Allow God to do His spiritual work of humbling you for his service.

3. The Lord may allow people to leave you because you have allowed your members to be ignorant by not teaching about loyalty and disloyalty.

> And with Absalom went two hundred men out of Jerusalem, that were called; and THEY WENT IN THEIR SIMPLICITY, and they knew not any thing.
>
> 2 Samuel 15:11

The devil feeds on the ignorance of the people. Deception always multiplies when people have not been exposed to the truth of the Word. Absalom was only able to lead two hundred men who went in the simplicity of their mind. This "simplicity of the mind" is what we also call ignorance.

The principles of loyalty and disloyalty, fatherhood and remembrance are often not taught in churches. No wonder the church members become easy prey to the demons of deception that feed on their ignorance. Perhaps you have allowed ignorance on these subjects to run rife in your congregation. Satan has taken advantage of their ignorance and wreaked havoc in your midst.

Yes, your congregation may be blessed with messages of prosperity, marriage and healing but none of these subjects adequately protect your congregation from the demons of disloyalty and treachery.

One day, a pastor asked me why I was teaching on loyalty and disloyalty. He mockingly remarked, "Loyalty is not something that is taught. It is something that you command."

He continued, "By your good character, you command the automatic loyalties of the people around you."

Shortly after this he was struck by the bitter experience of treachery from his own associates. He could not believe what was happening to him. After this experience, his despisement of my books and my teachings was converted into admiration. He became a fan of the subject of loyalty and began to promote my books himself. You may never know the importance of teaching until you experience the effects of ignorance.

4. **The Lord may allow people to leave you because you despised your fellow minister when his church split up.**

> ... he that is glad at calamities shall not be unpunished.
>
> Proverbs 17:5

Often, we despise people when they get into trouble. Like Job's friends, we seem to know the reasons for all the bad things that happen to people. We look down on people who are in trouble because we think they brought it upon themselves. This attitude can open the door for Satan to enter into our lives and ministry.

One day, I met up with three pastors of a super successful church. Their formidable team was made up of two strong associates and a senior pastor. With the help of his two associates, the senior pastor had successfully built one of the largest churches in the city. Everyone seemed to be flocking to their church. Their new church was bursting at its seams and they had multiple services with overflow crowds sitting outside. Filled with the exuberance of their recent successes they began to espouse theories as to why a sister church across town was not growing.

They said deridingly about the pastor of that church, "People only leave a church when it has a bad leader. It is because of his bad leadership that people have left his ministry and joined us."

At that time, I did not even know that people were leaving that other church and joining theirs. I was hearing for the first time that the other church had a "bad" leader. It was not difficult to sense a note of derision and mockery as they spoke about this church and its "bad" leader.

Yes, I do not doubt that people may have left the ministry because of its bad leadership. But you must be careful about how you come to your judgments and conclusions.

A couple of years later, these three leaders went through another phase in their ministry. Every new phase can bring about a change in the balance of power. In this new phase, the two associates left their senior pastor hurling insults and accusations at him. The exact thing for which they had despised the other pastor had happened to them but in a more severe way.

When I heard about this crisis, the first thing that occurred to me was what they had said about that sister church and its pastor, "People only leave you when you are a bad leader." Was their senior pastor now a bad leader? Not necessarily. There are many reasons why people may leave you. But make sure you do not mock at any one when he is in trouble.

In my country, there is a proverb which goes something like this: "When you see your friend's beard burning do not laugh at him. Do not ask how he could allow his beard to catch fire. Just go and fetch some water and keep it by your side in case yours also catches fire." The Bible puts it this way, "…he that is glad at calamities shall not be unpunished" (Proverbs 17:5).

5. The Lord may allow people to leave you because your destiny does not include them.

> Little children, it is the last time: and as ye have heard that antichrist shall come, even now are there many antichrists; whereby we know that it is the last time.
>
> THEY WENT OUT FROM US, BUT THEY WERE NOT OF US; for if they had been of us, they would no doubt have continued with us: but they went out, that they might be made manifest that they were not all of us.
>
> 1 John 2:18-19

Not everyone is called to be a part of your team. With our natural mind, we choose people that we feel should be with us. But God has already decided the people that are part of your destiny.

Through the years I have had the sad experience of having to let go of people whom I thought would be with me forever. I have also had the pleasant surprise of meeting their replacements. Honestly, I would not have chosen many of the people who are with me today. But God called them to help me fight in the ministry. Do not struggle when people are taken away from you. Sometimes it is in your eternal destiny that they be taken away and replaced with other people.

6. **The Lord may allow people to leave you so that you would understand how our heavenly father feels when His children leave Him.**

> And he said, A certain man had two sons: And the younger of them said to his father, Father, give me the portion of goods that falleth to me. And he divided unto them his living.
>
> And not many days after the younger son gathered all together, and took his journey into a far country, and there wasted his substance with riotous living.
>
> Luke 15:11-13

Becoming a father involves looking after all kinds of children. Sometimes, God will allow you to go through certain things so that you will mature into a father. You do not become a father because you are old. You become a father because you have children. You become a father because you can handle different kinds of children and the issues they present.

Cast your mind back to people like Jacob who had so many children. Each child was a different experience. Some children leave you unceremoniously as did the prodigal son. This is something that God experiences because He is the father of all of us. On your road to becoming a father, you are likely to experience people leaving you. Walking in love and maturity towards people who desert you suddenly, abandon you painfully and even turn against you is part of the process of becoming a father.

This is why God would allow some people to leave you – so that you can become a true father.

7. **The Lord may allow people to leave you to catch your attention and direct you to Him.**

> And the Lord was angry with Solomon, because his heart was turned from the Lord God of Israel, which had appeared unto him twice, and had commanded him concerning this thing, that he should not go after other gods: but he kept not that which the lord commanded. wherefore the Lord said unto Solomon, Forasmuch as this is done of thee, and THOU HAST NOT KEPT MY COVENANT AND MY STATUTES, which I have commanded thee, I WILL SURELY REND THE KINGDOM FROM THEE, AND WILL GIVE IT TO THY SERVANT.
>
> 1 Kings 11:9-11

Sometimes people leave you because you are out of the will of God. Jeroboam left the service of Solomon because Solomon was out of the will of God. Because the departure of someone is such a painful experience, it will not fail to get your attention.

Every time someone has left me, it has made me more prayerful and more spiritual. It has made me search myself and see whether I am in the will of God and whether I am doing the right thing. What carefulness, what clearing of myself and what fear it generates in my heart. "For behold this selfsame thing, that ye sorrowed after a godly sort, what carefulness it wrought in you, yea, what clearing of yourselves, yea, what indignation, yea, what fear, yea, what vehement desire, yea, what zeal, yea, what revenge! In all things ye have approved yourselves to be clear in this matter" (2 Corinthians 7:11).

You must also allow the departure of people to have this effect on you. The person may be a rebel but God will definitely use him to do a great spiritual work in you. If you are open, each person who leaves you will become a stepping stone to a higher dimension of ministry. I have a long list of people who have left me through the years. Of course, I have many more who have stayed with me. Indeed, I can tell you what I learnt from each and every single "departee".

8. The Lord may allow people to leave you because you have not continued to follow the Lord as you did at the beginning of your ministry.

He had seven hundred wives and three hundred concubines. And sure enough, they led his heart away from the Lord.

IN SOLOMON'S OLD AGE, THEY TURNED HIS HEART to worship their gods instead of trusting only in the Lord his God, as his father, David, had done."

1 Kings 11:3-4 (NLT)

Perhaps the most frightening aspect of people leaving you is the thought that you may be out of the will of God. Are you doing something that has opened the door of the enemy into your ministry? Is God pleased with you? Has the devil been allowed access because you have strayed outside His will? This must be one of your great considerations while praying about why someone has left you.

9. The Lord may allow people to leave you because you do not exert your authority.

You need to exert your authority and establish control over the people you lead. If you fail to exert your authority, all sorts of people will take you for granted. Weak leaders cannot establish loyalty in their churches. They allow people to exhibit dangerous signs of disloyalty without confronting them. Weak leaders gossip behind the backs of disloyal people instead of confronting them directly. This creates more confusion and more room for strife. In the end, the weak leader who does not want to confront people has a far worse crisis on his hand.

Solomon exerted his authority and eliminated his own brother Adonijah because he asked for Abishag (David's concubine) to become his wife.

You must notice subtle indicators of insolence, arrogance and presumption. It was Solomon's strength of character and his ability to exert authority that stabilised his kingdom. King Solomon was right when he reacted to the audacious request of Adonijah for Abishag. Notice Solomon's no-nonsense attitude towards Adonijah:

> Bath-sheba therefore went unto king Solomon, to speak unto him for Adonijah. And the king rose up to meet her, and bowed himself unto her, and sat down on his throne, and caused a seat to be set for the king's mother; and she sat on his right hand.
>
> Then she said, I desire one small petition of thee; I pray thee, say me not nay. And the king said unto her, Ask on, my mother: for I will not say thee nay.
>
> And she said, Let Abishag the Shunammite be given to Adonijah thy brother to wife.
>
> And king Solomon answered and said unto his mother, And why dost thou ask Abishag the Shunammite for Adonijah? Ask for him the kingdom also; for he is mine elder brother; even for him, and for Abiathar the priest, and for Joab the son of Zeruiah.
>
> Then king Solomon sware by the Lord, saying, God do so to me, and more also, if Adonijah have not spoken this word against his own life.
>
> Now therefore, as the Lord liveth, which hath established me, and set me on the throne of David my father, and who hath made me an house, as he promised, Adonijah shall be put to death this day.
>
> And king Solomon sent by the hand of Benaiah the son of Jehoiada; and he fell upon him that he died.
>
> 1 Kings 2:19-25

10. The Lord may allow people to leave you because you are too "hard".

> And the king answered the people roughly, and forsook the old men's counsel that they gave him; and spake to them

> after the counsel of the young men, saying, my father made your yoke heavy, and I will add to your yoke: my father also chastised you with whips, BUT I WILL CHASTISE YOU WITH SCORPIONS.
>
> 1 Kings 12:13-14

It is true that you must exert authority and demonstrate that you are in charge. Notice that Solomon did not simply exert authority because he was the king. He exerted his authority wisely and waited for good opportunities to establish his control.

Your actions must always appear rational and reasonable to the people around you. This helps them to accept your decisions and believe in your leadership.

11. The Lord may allow people to leave you because you are not a legitimate leader.

> And when Jehu was come to Jezreel, Jezebel heard of it; and she painted her face, and tired her head, and looked out at a window.
>
> And as Jehu entered in at the gate, she said, HAD ZIMRI PEACE, WHO SLEW HIS MASTER?
>
> 2 Kings 9:30-31

> And his servant Zimri, captain of half his chariots, conspired against him, as he was in Tirzah, drinking himself drunk in the house of Arza steward of his house in Tirzah.
>
> And Zimri went in and smote him, AND KILLED HIM, in the twenty and seventh year of Asa king of Judah, AND REIGNED IN HIS STEAD.
>
> 1 Kings 16:9-10

Zimri is the quintessential illegitimate leader. He had no right to be the king. He had no right to even desire the throne. Yet, he murdered the king and took over the throne. Unfortunately, his reign lasted only seven days. As you can see, illegitimate leaders have no stability.

Perhaps the most positive contribution of Jezebel to history is the question she asked the people who came to murder her. "Had Zimri peace, who slew his master?" In other words, did Zimri have a stable reign on the throne after slaying the legitimate leader? The answer is no. Jezebel tried to frighten off the murderers by reminding them of the inevitable fate of people who overthrow rightful leaders.

One of the chief reasons why people leave you is because you are not a legitimate leader. A legitimate leader is the rightful leader of a group. Rehoboam was the rightful king of Israel because he was the son of Solomon. Jeroboam was just a servant of Solomon. He had no legal rights to the throne of David and he knew it. Jeroboam knew that it was just a matter of time before the people would return and pay allegiance to the genuine and acceptable king of Israel. "And Jeroboam said in his heart, now shall the kingdom return to the house of David: If this people go up to do sacrifice in the house of the Lord at Jerusalem, THEN SHALL THE HEART OF THIS PEOPLE TURN AGAIN UNTO THEIR LORD, EVEN UNTO REHOBOAM KING OF JUDAH, and they shall kill me, and go again to Rehoboam king of Judah.

Whereupon the king took counsel, and made two calves of gold, and said unto them, It is too much for you to go up to Jerusalem: behold thy gods, O Israel, which brought thee up out of the land of Egypt" (1 Kings 12:26-28).

Jeroboam referred to Rehoboam as the lord of the people. He knew in his heart that Rehoboam was the legitimate king. It was this fear that the people would return to their legitimate king that made him set up idols in Dan and Bethel. When you break away half of someone's church and use it to start a church you are not the rightful leader of those people. Their rightful leader is the one whom they belonged to before you broke away.

When you break off someone's church and rename it you are not the rightful leader of the people.

When you lead a rebellion against your father and deceive a group of people to follow you, you are not the rightful leader of the group.

Why are you not the rightful leader of these groups? Because you didn't give birth to them but you stole them. Actually, you are not a leader but a thief and the curse of a thief will operate in your life. If your church is founded on rebellion and disloyalty, you are nothing more than a rebel. A rebel is not a rightful leader of anyone. This is why makers of coups become so brutal and murderous. When you are not a legitimate leader it is easy for people to turn against you and Jeroboam knew that very well. This is why illegitimate leaders often resort to mass murders and assassinations. Many African countries are led by illegitimate leaders who came into power through coups and civil wars. Their illegitimate authority is extended by murdering people and assassinating anyone perceived to be a threat. In the church world, illegitimate authority is difficult to maintain.

One day, I visited the branch church of a denomination which had been seized by the resident pastor. This pastor (who did not found the church), had painted over the name of the church and claimed ownership of something he did not own. As I stood in the church hall, I warned him that he was doing something wrong. I told him he could not steal someone's entire congregation. He did not agree with me and rather told me that God had given him a sign that He was with him. He took me outside to the car park and showed me a gleaming brand new car which someone had given to him as a gift for rebelling against his man of God. This pastor was determined to persist in becoming the illegitimate head of that church.

However, illegitimate authority is not easy to maintain. He was unable to control the associates, the elders and the congregation. After a short while the church and its pastors rose up and threw him out of the church.

On another occasion, I was invited to preach in a church somewhere in Ghana. I realised that this church was not growing.

The pastor was experiencing break-ups and splits in the church all the time. He did not understand what was happening. "Why isn't my church growing?" he asked. Some of the prominent members of his church had just left and he was devastated.

"What is going on?" he asked. "Every time I take two steps forward it seems I take three steps backwards."

In a flash, I remembered how he began his church. He had been an associate pastor for many years and one day he left his senior pastor with a large section of the congregation along with the most prominent members of the church. Actually, he had gone along with the pastor's main supporter and financier. His senior pastor's main financier had become his chief supporter. Obviously, he was not a legitimate leader of these people and yet he wanted to build a stable, loyal and growing congregation with these stolen people. For several years, he endured one breakaway after another, never able to gain stable control of the little congregation. It is important that you are the legitimate captain of your ship.

12. The Lord may allow people to leave you because they saw you leave others and learnt from what you did.

People leave you because they learnt it from you. People eventually do what they see you do. This is why David refused to kill Saul. If David had killed Saul, he would have set the precedent for killing kings. Saul had made a mistake and was now demon-possessed and sleeping in witches' homes. But, it was only a matter of time before David would make equally grave mistakes deserving the same punishment. Perhaps, the one thing that should guide your actions most is that the people around you are learning from what you do. Notice how Zimri the captain of the chariots overthrew king Elah and reigned in his stead. Shortly after that, the people rose up to eliminate Zimri and make Omri, the captain of the host the king.

Zimri Overthrows the King

And his SERVANT ZIMRI, captain of half his chariots, CONSPIRED AGAINST HIM, as he was in Tirzah, drinking himself drunk in the house of Arza steward of his house in Tirzah.

And Zimri went in and smote him, and killed him, in the twenty and seventh year of Asa king of Judah, and reigned in his stead.

1 Kings 16:9-10

The People Overthrow Zimri

In the twenty and seventh year of Asa king of Judah did Zimri reign seven days in Tirzah. And the people were encamped against...

And THE PEOPLE THAT WERE ENCAMPED HEARD say, Zimri hath conspired, and hath also slain the king: wherefore all Israel made Omri, the captain of the host, king over Israel that day in the camp. And Omri went up from Gibbethon, and all Israel with him, and they besieged Tirzah.

And it came to pass, when Zimri saw that the city was taken, that he went into the palace of the king's house, and burnt the king's house over him with fire, and died, For his sins which he sinned in doing evil in the sight of the Lord, in walking in the way of Jeroboam, and in his sin which he did, to make Israel to sin.

1 Kings 16:15-19

13. The Lord may allow people to leave you because you lack wisdom and leadership skills.

Foolish leadership can undo years of hard work and building. An unwise person at the helm of affairs is a disaster waiting to happen. Solomon predicted the arrival of a foolish son called Rehoboam. "Thus I hated all the fruit of my labor for which I had labored under the sun, for I must leave it to the man who will come after me.

And who knows whether he will be a wise man or a fool? YET HE WILL HAVE CONTROL OVER ALL THE FRUIT OF MY LABOR FOR WHICH I HAVE LABORED BY ACTING WISELY UNDER THE SUN. This too is vanity" (Ecclesiastes 2:18-19, NASB).

Solomon knew that a fool on his throne would dissipate and disperse all that he had suffered to build. Indeed he was right. With the arrival of one foolish leader the greatest accumulation of wealth and the richest estate ever known to man was dispersed.

Perhaps even more tragically, the foolish son dispersed the kingdom itself. Within the first few months of taking over the kingdom, he took unwise decisions that led to the complete break-up of the family of Israel. Israel has never been the same since the era of Rehoboam.

I know you may not want to admit it, but it may be your lack of wisdom that is the cause of the continuous breakup of your church. It may be your inability to manage and lead wisely that cause people to leave you.

One day, I noticed how hundreds of people had gathered at the embassies of the European and American countries.

I asked myself, "Why do so many people want to leave Africa? Why do so many people want to leave for Europe? Is it because of bad weather in Africa? Is the weather better in Europe?"

The answer is "no"!

They want to escape from the bad leadership that is prevalent in the African world. They want to live their lives under a different kind of leadership – and you can't really blame them for that. Who wouldn't want to escape from a harsh unforgiving world ruled by leaders who lack the wisdom to create peace, stability, wealth and prosperity for their people?

This is what happens when people leave churches. They are running away from our bad and inconsiderate leadership. They are escaping from a church ruled by leaders who lack the wisdom to create peace, stability, wealth and prosperity for their members! Your associate pastors may leave you because they are desperately trying to get away from your poor and unwise leadership. I got you there!

14. The Lord may allow people to leave you as a judgment on your life.

There are times that the departure of people is allowed by the Lord as a judgment for your sins. This may be confusing because we all know that God hates rebellion.

The effect of rebellion is devastating and that is why God sometimes uses it as a judgment. But, please also note that the people who rise up in rebellion are later judged themselves for having rebelled.

Because of Jeroboam's grave sins, God allowed a conspirator called Baasha to successfully rebel and wipe out the entire family of Jeroboam.

Later on however, the Lord equally judged Baasha for his rebellion. Zimri was then raised up to rebel and destroy the kingdom of Baasha.

Baasha Destroys Nadab as a Judgment against Jeroboam

> And Nadab the son of Jeroboam began to reign over Israel in the second year of Asa king of Judah, and reigned over Israel two years. And he did evil in the sight of the Lord, and walked in the way of his father, and in his sin wherewith he made Israel to sin.
>
> And BAASHA THE SON OF AHIJAH, OF THE HOUSE OF ISSACHAR, CONSPIRED AGAINST HIM; AND BAASHA SMOTE HIM AT GIBBETHON, which belonged to the Philistines; for Nadab and all Israel laid siege to Gibbethon.

Even in the third year of Asa king of Judah did Baasha slay him, and reigned in his stead.

And it came to pass, when he reigned, that HE SMOTE ALL THE HOUSE OF JEROBOAM; he left not to Jeroboam any that breathed, until he had destroyed him, according unto the saying of the Lord, which he spake by his servant Ahijah the Shilonite:

BECAUSE OF THE SINS OF JEROBOAM which he sinned, and which he made Israel sin, by his provocation wherewith he provoked the Lord God of Israel to anger.

1 Kings 15:25-30

Zimri Destroys Baasha as a Judgment against Baasha

And it came to pass, when he began to reign, as soon as he sat on his throne, that he slew all the house of Baasha: he left him not one that pisseth against a wall, neither of his kinsfolks, nor of his friends.

THUS DID ZIMRI DESTROY ALL THE HOUSE OF BAASHA, according to the word of the Lord, which he spake against Baasha by Jehu the prophet,

FOR ALL THE SINS OF BAASHA, AND THE SINS OF ELAH HIS SON, by which they sinned, and by which they made Israel to sin, in provoking the Lord God of Israel to anger with their vanities.

1 Kings 16:11-13

15. The Lord may allow people to leave you because you are not quick to deal with disloyalty.

Because the sentence against an evil deed is not executed quickly, therefore the hearts of the sons of men among them are given fully to do evil.

Ecclesiastes 8:11 (NASB)

Disloyalty is a spiritual emergency. It must be dealt with quickly before it grows and pollutes the rest of the people. There are many sayings which allude to this fact – "one bad apple spoils the bunch"; "a little leaven leaveneth the whole lump" are just a couple of these.

Disloyalty is a polluting and contaminating situation which changes the nature of everything and everyone. It is important that you deal with it as quickly as possible. Otherwise everything in your ministry will change.

When people are bitten by a cobra, they begin running immediately. They run for miles trying to make it to the nearest hospital before the poison kills them. Their only hope is to get to the hospital before the venom kills them.

Such is the nature of poison and such is the nature of disloyalty. It is an emergency! You cannot allow your congregation to be polluted by the negative attitude of disloyal leaders. You cannot allow people who exhibit all the signs of disloyalty to move around unchecked. You cannot afford to do this!

Solomon was quick to deal with disloyalty. That is why he executed his uncle, Joab, his brother, Adonijah and Shimei at the very first opportunity. He knew it was dangerous to leave these people. He knew it was dangerous to accommodate men who had shown the desire to overthrow him.

Perhaps it is your SLOWNESS at dealing with disloyalty that has allowed disloyal people to have their way in your ministry. Read for yourself how Solomon dealt quickly with three dangerous elements in his kingdom: Adonijah, Joab and Shimei.

Solomon Deals Quickly with Adonijah

> And king Solomon answered and said unto his mother, And why dost thou ask Abishag the Shunammite for Adonijah? ask for him the kingdom also; for he is mine elder brother; even for him, and for Abiathar the priest, and for Joab the son of Zeruiah.

Then king Solomon sware by the Lord, saying, God do so to me, and more also, if Adonijah have not spoken this word against his own life.
Now therefore, as the Lord liveth, which hath established me, and set me on the throne of David my father, and who hath made me an house, as he promised, Adonijah shall be put to death this day.
And king Solomon sent by the hand of Benaiah the son of Jehoiada; and he fell upon him that he died.

1 Kings 2:22-25

Solomon Deals Quickly with Joab

And it was told king Solomon that Joab was fled unto the tabernacle of the Lord; and, behold, he is by the altar. Then Solomon sent Benaiah the son of Jehoiada, saying, Go, fall upon him.

1 Kings 2:29

Solomon Deals Quickly with Shimei

The king said moreover to Shimei, Thou knowest all the wickedness which thine heart is privy to, that thou didst to David my father: therefore the Lord shall return thy wickedness upon thine own head;

And king Solomon shall be blessed, and the throne of David shall be established before the Lord for ever.

So the king commanded Benaiah the son of Jehoiada; which went out, and fell upon him, that he died. And the kingdom was established in the hand of Solomon.

1 Kings 2:44-46

CHAPTER 2

Demons That Operate in Those Who Leave in Rebellion

1. The spirit of Lucifer operates in those who leave in rebellion.

> How art thou fallen from heaven, O Lucifer, son of the morning! How art thou cut down to the ground, which didst weaken the nations!
>
> For thou hast said in thine heart, I WILL ASCEND into heaven, I WILL EXALT my throne above the stars of God: I will sit also upon the mount of the congregation, in the sides of the north:
>
> I WILL ASCEND above the heights of the clouds; I will be like the most High.
>
> Yet thou shalt be brought down to hell, to the sides of the pit.
>
> Isaiah 14:12-15

The spirit of Lucifer is the spirit that moves out of place and out of rank! Satan is the archetypal rebel who left the service of God and became an enemy. He has since then inspired all rebels and leavers. Satan's prime/principal aim is to destabilise the church you are building and destroy the work of God.

The best way he can do it is to poison your leadership team and give them reasons to leave you. Satan is the spirit of destruction and he has targeted the pillars of your church. Satan desperately wants to pull down your "spiritual building" and he knows that if he can bring down the pillars, the whole building will come crashing down. This is why he targets your associate pastors, your co-workers and your important people.

This is why you must focus on your leaders. Satan is focusing on them whether you believe it or not. He is working hard to poison them and to turn them against you. He is working hard to sow the seeds of doubt, fear and confusion in the people you trust most. Satan is working on the hearts of the people who are most important to your mission. You better rise up and teach them the things that will stabilise their hearts.

Intruder in the Night

One of my pastors shared an important vision with me. In this vision, he was asleep in his bed at home in the middle of the night. An intruder came through the window and walked up to his sleeping figure on the bed. When the intruder got to his body, the intruder opened what looked like a door in his chest, put something inside it and ran out of the window. This intruder was no other person than Satan. God had revealed to this brother that Satan would try to plant something in his heart. God was warning him to be careful about seeds that Satan could sow in his spirit.

This vision clearly illustrated to me that Satan was at work trying to poison the hearts of the people that I was leading.

Because Lucifer is basically a rebel, he inspires all rebellions. Every time you fight disloyalty and rebellion you are fighting Satan directly.

Because Lucifer is the embodiment of all rebellion, teachings on loyalty and disloyalty are direct attacks on his presence in a church or ministry.

Go to the root of the matter and deal with Satan in your church by confronting disloyalty and teaching your people to be loyal.

2. **The spirit of false prophecy operates in those who leave in rebellion.**

And the Lord said, who shall persuade Ahab, that he may go up and fall at Ramoth-gilead? And one said on this manner, and another said on that manner. And there came forth a spirit, and stood before the Lord, and said, I will persuade him.

1 Kings 22:20-21

Many people do things because a prophet tells them to do it. It is important to ensure that you are following the voice of the Lord when you obey a prophetic word. In this classic story, Ahab followed the voice of the false prophet and he was led to his destruction. The spirit of false prophecy actually persuaded him to go and fall at Ramothgilead. This is what happens to rebellious people. They are actually persuaded by the devil to go to their doom and destruction.

The Spirit of False Prophecy

Many rebels justify their actions with prophecies. In the name of the Holy Spirit, they rise up and do the work of Satan, destroying churches and causing confusion in the vineyard of the Lord. Only God can tell whether they are sent by a spirit of prophecy or a spirit of false prophecy.

Higher Dimensions

I once had a pastor who was a national of a neighbouring African country. This pastor had been faithful to me, working in a European city and pastoring one of our churches. One day, he went on vacation to his country. Whilst visiting a church conference, a "man of God" came up to him and told him, "I see you moving into higher dimensions." He said that he had not met this "higher dimensions" prophet before and was surprised that he would say those words to him. That prophecy was the seed of rebellion sown into this man's heart.

From that moment, my faithful pastor began to consider "higher dimensions" of ministry. A year or two later, he went back on another home visit. Yet again he met this prophet who asked him whether he had moved into "higher dimensions". Upon hearing that, my faithful pastor broke his shining record of faithfulness and decided to join a long list of rebellious leavers.

Because of this "prophetic word", this pastor began to conspire with the congregation to leave our denomination. By the time I became aware of his resignation the deed was done and he had won the hearts of most of the congregation. He then took away ninety percent of the congregation and started his own independent church. In the end, our church had to actually close down because there was no one left in it. Through this "prophecy" an entire church had been shut down.

I have but one question to ask: Is the Holy Spirit breaking down the Church or is He building it up? He is building it. Jesus said, "I will build my church." He did not say, "I will destroy my church."

Is it not a sin to build something which you have just destroyed? What does the Bible say? Why do you utterly destroy one church only to build another? How can you spend five years of your life building a church and then destroy it utterly? How can you spend years of your life building a congregation and then turn around to disperse and scatter the sheep? What are their motives? Are these people looking for money? Are they looking for power? What does the Scripture say?

> **For if I build again the things which I destroyed, I make myself a transgressor.**
>
> **Galatians 2:18**

I do not believe that this gentleman followed a prophet. It is indeed possible that he actually followed a demon and a false prophet. God will one day reveal whether this pastor followed a demon, a false prophet or the Holy Spirit. The Bible teaches us to beware of false prophets and false prophecies. False prophets and false prophecies are the way to perish.

> **For I have not sent them, saith the Lord, yet they prophesy a lie in my name; that I might drive you out, and that ye might PERISH, ye, and the prophets that prophesy unto you.**
>
> **Jeremiah 27:15**

3. The spirit of greed operates in those who leave in rebellion.

> **FEED THE FLOCK OF GOD which is among you, taking the oversight thereof, not by constraint, but willingly; NOT FOR FILTHY LUCRE, but of a ready mind;**
>
> **1 Peter 5:2**

Apostle Peter knew very well that many ministers would feed the flock of God for the sake of money. And he said it plainly, "Feed the flock of God and not for filthy lucre!"

Money is the Root of all Breakaways

Money is the root of all evil. From my little experience, almost all breakaway situations in churches have their roots in money. The evil that enters churches destroying and dividing them has its roots in money. Let me give you some homework to do. Carefully analyse these people who leave in anger and rebellion. You will be amazed to find out that almost all those who leave you are money-hungry covetous men. They may have left accusing you of terrible sins but they are just looking for money. Sadly, many of our decisions are driven by our desperation to have money or to have the control of money.

Gehazi is the pastor who lost his ministry because of his desire for money. Most of us will not admit our base desire for more and more money. Unfortunately, many decisions are driven by the desire for money.

Look at what happened to Gehazi, the servant of Elisha the prophet. His master refused to receive money from Naaman, the Syrian. Out of greed, Gehazi went ahead, lied to him and took the money for himself.

By this act, Gehazi dishonoured the ministry of Elisha. Elisha cursed Gehazi and instead of becoming a prophet, Gehazi became a leper.

> **The leprosy therefore of Naaman shall cleave unto thee, and unto thy seed for ever. And he went out from his presence a leper as white as snow.**
>
> **2 Kings 5:27**

Some people are not called to be heads, but they want to be heads. They look with greed at the things their superiors have. They look with greedy eyes at the cars and houses which their bosses have! Some people would not even be satisfied if they were given your wife. They do not just want what you have. They actually want to be you! Some people are so greedy that they want nothing but to replace you. They want to be you!

The Bible says, "Beware of covetousness." The prodigal son had everything at home. Do you remember what he said in his time of need? He declared that even the servants in his father's house had more than enough to eat.

Discontentment and greed drove him out of a place where he had everything. He was inspired by demons to seek after non-existent fantasies.

Whenever someone is led by evil spirits, he ends up in a dark and barren land. It is the Lord who leads people to green pastures. It is the devil who leads people to the place of desolation.

> **And he said unto them, Take heed, and beware of covetousness: for a man's life consisteth not in the abundance of the things which he possesseth.**
>
> **Luke 12:15**

Do you have the spirit of greed? Let Apostle Paul's admonition guide you and deliver you from this destructive spirit of greed:

> **But godliness with contentment is great gain. For we brought nothing into this world, and it is certain we can carry nothing out. And having food and raiment let us be therewith content.**
>
> **1 Timothy 6:6-8**

4. The independent spirit operates in those who leave in rebellion.

> **And he said, A certain man had two sons: And the younger of them said to his father, Father, GIVE ME THE PORTION OF GOODS THAT FALLETH TO ME. And he divided unto them his living.**
>
> **Luke 15:11-13**

There are people who only think of how they may become independent. I do believe in independence, but not all independence is good. Independence that kills or destroys the rest of the body is evil. Independence that is premature is evil. Independence that is achieved without due honour to the parents is evil.

The Independent Spirit is the Spirit of Cancer

Perhaps the most deadly form of rebellion is found in people who have an independent spirit. The revelation of what an independent spirit is can be best understood by understanding what cancer is. Cancer occurs when a small part of the body decides to independently develop. Cancer of the breast, cancer of the stomach, cancer of the rectum, cancer of the brain kills the bodies of their victims by their independence.

People with the independent spirit cause great confusion in churches and leadership teams. Their independent attitudes and activities are awkward because they cause confusion and uncertainty in the body. The rest of the body does not know how to respond to their independent moves. Can you imagine how the body feels because it is uncertain whether the breast intends to kill the rest of the body? Should we keep this breast on or should we cut it off? Indeed, it takes a clever and detailed microscopic analysis to know whether the independence of a part of the breast is going to kill the rest of the body. Indeed, it is not easy to identify and deal with dangerous and life-threatening independent spirits.

Premature Independence

In the womb, the baby is totally dependent on its mother for survival. In the womb, the baby is linked to its mother. This total dependence does not last forever. It only lasts for nine months. It is important for the baby to become disconnected from its mother at a point. Nature itself teaches us about the need for independence. However, if this baby becomes independent too early, it will actually die.

This should serve as a strong warning to those who just crave for independence at any time. Also, cutting the cord between the mother and the baby in the wrong way can lead to severe life-threatening infections for the baby.

Independence that Dishonours Parents

This fact also illustrates that acquiring independence in the wrong way can also kill you. You cannot acquire your independence without giving due honour to your parents. A child who walks away from his parents in anger and rebellion is setting himself up for destruction. A child who despises the home which raised him up will be destroyed. A child who becomes independent and forgets how he was cared for and loved dishonours his parents.

Independence that is acquired in the wrong way and at the wrong time is evil. Independence that is acquired with the wrong motives is also evil.

Some pastors, who have become independent when God did not send them, are finding out that it is not that easy to be independent.

I remember one rebellious pastor who left his home church breathing threats and curses. He boasted, "Give me six months, and I will show you all about church growth!" He spoke of the great things he would accomplish now that he was on his own.

However, as the years went by, like the prodigal boy, he found out that life and ministry are more complex than they look! The spirit of "evil independence" is the spirit that leads a person to independence but in an evil way. Independence is a good thing if it is inspired, engineered and directed by God.

People who leave and acquire "evil independence" often appear successful very quickly. The spirit of "evil independence" looks for flashy, quick and instantly successful things. But the man who built his house on the rock will necessarily be slower than the man who built his house on the sand. Do not be attracted to the emptiness of temporary successes.

Godly Spiritual Independence

The apostle Paul was independent. He said he consulted no one. Read his words:

> **For I neither received it of man, neither was I taught it ... I conferred not with flesh and blood:**
>
> **Galatians 1:12, 16**

Paul is telling us here that as far as his ministry is concerned, he is independent of all men. Timothy, however, was not independent. Paul wrote to Timothy and told him exactly what to do and exactly what to preach. When you read the book of Timothy, you will notice that it is full of instructions from Paul. In ministry, Timothy was dependent on Paul. Paul gave him many instructions for ministry. Notice a few of these:

Let no man despise thy youth; but be thou an example of the believers, in word, in conversation, in charity, in spirit, in faith, in purity. Till I come, give attendance to reading, to exhortation, to doctrine.

Neglect not the gift that is in thee, which was given thee by prophecy, with the laying on of the hands of the presbytery. Meditate upon these things; give thyself wholly to them; that thy profiting may appear to all.

Take heed unto thyself, and unto the doctrine; continue in them: for in doing this thou shalt both save thyself, and them that hear thee.

1 Timothy 4:12-16

Thou therefore, my son, be strong in the grace that is in Christ Jesus. And the things that thou hast heard of me among many witnesses, the same commit thou to faithful men, who shall be able to teach others also.

2 Timothy 2:1-2

Independence, when it is God's command, is a beautiful thing but when it is not of God, it leads to destruction and death. People who leave their God-given positions to acquire independence often fade away and become frustrated. Many so-called "independent" churches acquired their independence in the wrong way and at the wrong time.

5. The spirit of foolishness operates in those who leave in rebellion.

Some people leave their positions because they are afflicted with the spirit of foolishness. Foolishness is the opposite of wisdom. Taking unwise decisions that lead to desolation and poverty are the hallmarks of a fool. Why should you take a decision that destroys your life?

It is difficult to fathom why people do certain things. But in life, many people take foolish decisions which destroy them. Foolishness and stubbornness are sisters. A foolish person is usually stubborn and unyielding. A fool's reaction to advice will often give him away. In fact, a fool will hate you for giving him sound advice. This is a cardinal feature of the spirit of foolishness.

I am sure that many people spoke to the prodigal son about his decision to leave. Perhaps his father, mother, uncles and aunties tried to advice him. The spirit of foolishness makes you deaf to advice and counsel.

... fools despise wisdom and instruction.

Proverbs 1:7

But ye have set at nought all my counsel, and would none of my reproof:

Proverbs 1:25

The spirit of foolishness makes you hate advice. It makes you hate your counsellor. When you shut out godly advice and counsel from your life, you shut the door to great opportunities and blessings!

Do you have feelings of resentment towards your pastors? Do you get angry with the people who advice you? Then perhaps you have the spirit of foolishness!

Stubbornness and rebellion are also related ills. You often find rebellion somewhere in the company of stubbornness. "And they shall say unto the elders of his city, this our son is STUBBORN AND REBELLIOUS, he will not obey our voice; he is a glutton, and a drunkard" (Deuteronomy 21:20). Stalin, the leader of Russia who caused the deaths of millions of his own people, was known to be a stubborn person. He was dismissed from Bible School for his stubborn views. Hitler, another mass murderer, was also known for his stubbornness in his childhood.

The triple action syndrome of foolishness, stubbornness and rebellion can be found in most people who cause divisions and church splits.

People who leave churches unceremoniously destroying whatever they can on their way out are often possessed by this triple action demon – foolishness, stubbornness and rebellion.

6. **The spirit of selfishness operates in those who leave in rebellion.**

And as for you, My flock, thus says the Lord God, Behold, I will judge between one sheep and another, between the rams and the male goats.

Is it too slight a thing for you that you should feed in the good pasture, that you MUST TREAD DOWN WITH YOUR FEET THE REST OF YOUR PASTURES? or that you should drink of the clear waters, that you must foul the rest with your feet?

And as for my flock, they must eat what you tread down with your feet, and they must drink what you foul with your feet!

Ezekiel 34:17-19 (NASB)

People who leave you are often selfish. A selfish person does not care what happens to other people. He is only concerned that he does well for himself.

When the prodigal son left home he must have caused much embarrassment to his family. Friends must have asked his father, "We hear your son is feeding with pigs across the desert. Is it true?"

Can you imagine the questions that were raised by this boy's actions? What happened? Why did he leave? What was going on at home? Why did he ask for his inheritance? Was his father being cruel to him? Was there any child abuse going on?

Can you imagine the rumours that were rife in the city?

I hear the two sons are from different mothers.

I hear the family is breaking up.

I hear the father is a very difficult man to live with.

But the prodigal son did not care what anybody thought. He did not mind if people had a bad impression about his father.

This selfish attitude can be found in many "leavers".

I remember blessing a particular pastor after he informed me that he was leaving. I was amazed at how he turned against me after his departure.

No, he did not leave quietly. He spread false stories about the church and caused me a lot of problems. Because of this gentleman, I rarely pray for people when they inform me that they are leaving. I now wait to see how they behave after they have left.

There are many ministers who do not care about what happens to the church that nurtured them. Though they benefited from it for years, they do not mind destroying it when they are angry.

> **For if I build again the things which I destroyed, I make myself a TRANSGRESSOR.**
>
> **Galatians 2:18**

These selfish people now prevent others from benefiting from what they have benefited from over the years. "Seemeth it a small thing...to have eaten up the good pasture, but ye must tread down with your feet the residue of your pastures..." (Ezekiel 34:18).

How can you eat up all the good pasture and then tread on the rest of it?

What are the others going to eat? Do not be selfish!

Is it a small thing for you to drink of the clear waters and after that excrete into the rest of it? What are the others going to drink?

There are people who have drunk from the pulpit of a church for several years. When they decide to leave the church, they cause a stir and say so many things that damage the reputation of the church and its pastor.

When such selfish people leave a church, the rest of the congregation usually becomes confused. They cannot tell if they are in a good church or not – or whether they have a good pastor or not. Woe to those who selfishly trample on the pastures that others could feed on.

Everybody grew up somewhere. I grew up in different groups. I belonged to a Christian group called "Calvary Road Incorporated". I learnt a lot of my ministry skills from this group, and I am grateful to them for this. Now I do not belong to this group anymore. But the fact that I do not belong there anymore does not mean I should destroy them.

It is the pasture from which I grew up! It is the water from which I drank!

Is it a small thing then, for me to eat of a pasture and after that trample it down, so that nobody else can enjoy it?

Is it a small thing to drink of the waters and afterwards urinate into it - so that nobody else can drink from it?

But that is exactly what people do when they leave churches. They say evil things about the place they came from.

Has somebody been a father to you and nurtured you in the ministry?

Then remember that you are not the only child he will ever nurture. There will be others who must be nurtured by this same man of God.

Do not urinate in the water you just drank from. Do not urinate on your father. Do not defaecate in the front door as you walk out of the church. Do not leave a foul and uncertain smell as you depart angrily.

If you want to leave - please just leave! Go quietly and pray for a blessing.

7. **The spirit of deception operates in those who leave in rebellion.**

And when the thousand years are expired, Satan shall be loosed out of his prison, and SHALL GO OUT TO DECEIVE the nations which are in the four quarters of the earth, Gog and Magog, TO GATHER THEM TOGETHER TO BATTLE....

Revelation 20:7-8

Most conflicts have an evil spirit behind them. The spirit of Satan is the spirit that gathers the people of God and sets them up in conflict against each other. You will notice from the Scripture above that as soon as Satan was released from prison he gathered people to fight and kill each other. Satan is able to get people to fight against each other through deception.

It is the spirit of deception that turns us against each other. When the Holy Spirit is in you, you will not turn against your father and your brothers. When the spirit of Satan is operating through you, you will do battle with your fathers and brothers in the ministry.

How you conduct yourself when you leave reveals the kind of spirit you carry.

8. **The spirit of ungratefulness operates in those who leave in rebellion.**

Whoso rewardeth evil for good, evil shall not depart from his house.

Proverbs 17:13

Many people who leave are possessed by the spirit of ingratitude. They do not remember the many things that have been done for them over the years. Most people do not appreciate what has been done for them. Actually, most people do not even think that anything has been done for them! If people would remember what was done for them, they would behave very differently.

As a father, I now understand what my parents went through for many years in order to give me what I have. Never repay evil to somebody who has been good to you – be it your pastor, mother, father, stepmother, stepfather, or whoever.

Jeremiah suffered at the hands of ungrateful people. Jeremiah asked whether evil was the reward for doing good. He complained to God that his church members had dug a pit for his soul. Then he reminded God that he had interceded many times for them. Then he cursed them!

Shall evil be recompensed for good?
Jeremiah 18:20a

... Remember that I stood before thee to speak good for them, and to turn away thy wrath from them.
Jeremiah 18:20b

Therefore deliver up their children ... and pour out their blood ... Let a cry be heard from their houses ... forgive not their iniquity ... Shall evil be recompensed for good?
Jeremiah 18:21-23, 20

The Bible makes it clear that curses follow ungrateful people. People are generally ungrateful.

Some children grow up and then insult and mistreat their parents. But whether your mother is a prostitute or not, she is still your mother. Whether your father is a criminal or not he is your father! Respect them and be grateful to them for bringing you into this world.

All ministers of the gospel should know that people are generally ungrateful. You are naive when you think that people will appreciate your efforts.

Jesus knew it! He experienced it! One time, after an angry crowd tried to kill Jesus, He asked:

... Many good works have I shewed you from my Father; FOR WHICH OF THOSE WORKS DO YE STONE ME?

John 10:32

9. The spirit of pride operates in those who leave in rebellion.

By the multitude of thy merchandise they have filled the midst of thee with violence, and thou hast sinned: therefore I will cast thee as profane out of the mountain of God: and I will destroy thee, O covering cherub, from the midst of the stones of fire.

THINE HEART WAS LIFTED UP because of thy beauty, thou hast corrupted thy wisdom by reason of thy brightness: I will cast thee to the ground, I will lay thee before kings, that they may behold thee.

Thou hast defiled thy sanctuaries by the multitude of thine iniquities, by the iniquity of thy traffick; therefore will I bring forth a fire from the midst of thee, it shall devour thee, and I will bring thee to ashes upon the earth in the sight of all them that behold thee.

Ezekiel 28:16-18

Satan's Children Are the Children of Pride

The spirit of Satan is the spirit of pride. Perhaps the commonest spirit that operates in "leavers" is the spirit of pride. Satan is the greatest example of the rebellious "leaver." Satan is also the spirit of pride that exalts itself against the throne of God. The spirit of pride vaunts itself and challenges legitimate authorities. Satan's children are the children of pride.

He beholdeth all high *things:* he (leviathan) is a king over all the children of pride.

Job 41:34

The children of pride have the spirit that corrects upwards. Correction upwards is rebellion, and Satan is the spirit of rebellion. The children of pride have the spirit that thoughtlessly rebukes and corrects authorities, fathers and holy men of God.

The children of pride speak in a particular way. Arrogance and presumption ooze out of them when they speak.

One day, I met a pastor who had worked with me for several years but had left to form his own church. We talked for a few minutes during which he made several angry but classic statements. He said:

"I don't need you and you don't need me"

Only the children of pride will say something like, "I don't need you and you don't need me."

It is pride that makes people think they don't need anyone. After all they are big enough to survive on their own! But we need each other and we will never be perfect without each other (Hebrews 11:40).

Another pastor who had worked with me for several years and had also left to start his own church said to me:

"I don't owe you anything"

But he owed me his very life and did not even know it. I could not believe it, as this forgetful fellow confidently explained how he did not have any obligations towards me. Of course, a debtor is subject to the lender. It was another way of telling me that he was no longer subject to me. Pride is what makes people feel big and talk big. It is also the spirit that inspires them to defiantly walk away from you.

On another occasion, I visited a rebellious pastor and tried to reconcile with him but he would have none of it. In anger he asked us to leave and said:

"Next time you are coming, come with more *sense*"

But what could be more sensible than trying to reconcile with your brother? Are we not commanded to love one another and to forgive each other? Are we not instructed to leave our offering at the altar and go back to reconcile with our brothers?

On yet another occasion, I sent for a pastor who had become puffed up by his recent successes in ministry. He was getting ready to present his resignation letter and launch out on his own. You see, for the first time he had experienced the joy of church growth and the thrill of a successful teaching ministry. People were after his messages and wanted to buy all his tapes, CDs and DVDs. I asked him to come for a meeting but he sent me a message saying:

"Tell him I will not come"

Time and time again, you see pride exuding from these "leavers". The children of pride give themselves away by the way they speak. The children of pride are carrying the spirit of Leviathan, the spirit of Lucifer; the chiefest and first among all rebels.

10. The spirit of wickedness operates in those who leave in rebellion.

And one told David, saying, Ahithophel is among the conspirators with Absalom. And David said, O Lord, I pray thee, turn the counsel of Ahithophel into foolishness.

2 Samuel 15:31

Moreover Ahithophel said unto Absalom, Let me now choose out twelve thousand men, and I will arise and pursue after David this night: And I will come upon him while he is weary and weak handed, and will make him afraid: and all the people that are with him shall flee; and I will smite the king only.

2 Samuel 17:1-2

Ahithophel was the counsellor and friend of King David. He turned against him and offered to lead an army of twelve thousand men to assassinate his old friend. When someone moves against you in a way that will destroy you and everything that you stand for, that person is anointed with the spirit of wickedness.

Many people who leave churches are anointed with this spirit of wickedness. They think their departure will finish you. And that is what they want. They are often surprised when you continue to flourish after they have done their worst.

She Thought She Could Finish Him Off

One day, the wife of a great American prophet decided to leave her husband. She claimed he had no time for her emotional needs. The pastor begged his wife not to leave but she would not listen. Finally, when the die was cast, the lawyers were called in to work out the terms of the separation. The wife demanded a huge amount to be paid to compensate her. Then she struck her final blow and demanded that the entire sum be paid to her before the church be informed of the divorce.

Obviously, she thought that the announcement of the divorce would destroy the reputation of her husband. With her husband's reputation destroyed, she knew that the church would suffer huge financial setbacks and probably not be able to pay her.

Even though she knew that her move would destroy her husband, she went right ahead and divorced him. She did not care whether her husband or the church was destroyed. It is the spirit of wickedness that leads people to make moves to wipe you out and terminate your ministry! Somehow he survived and continued to prophesy the Word of God.

Miracle Man Was Wrong!

A great evangelist once had an associate minister called Miracle Man. This associate minister had the unique job of praying for the sick at every crusade. After the evangelist had finished preaching his powerful Gospel message, this associate would come on the stage to pray for the sick.

One day, Miracle Man decided to leave the ministry unceremoniously. The evangelist was shocked and disappointed at the departure of this man whom he had depended on for a long time. At the next crusade however, the evangelist was forced to pray for the sick himself. Although he was scared and intimidated, he went ahead and began to successfully minister to the sick.

After the crusade, the evangelist overheard one of his workers saying, "Miracle Man was wrong."

So the evangelist asked, "Why do you say Miracle Man was wrong?"

The brother confessed, "Before Miracle Man left he said, 'When I leave, the evangelist is finished.' But I realize that Miracle Man was wrong. You are not finished. The ministry has continued in power, strength and glory."

Indeed, disloyal people are wicked people. They think they can take a step which will wipe you out and silence you forever. O how disappointed they are when they see you moving forward and going further. They secretly find out more about you on the internet and watch you on television, completely amazed that you are doing even better without them.

Pastors who toy with disloyal people do not know that disloyal people are also wicked people.

Believe me dear friend; *there is a disloyal and wicked spirit that would love to wipe you out.* There is a spirit that is postured to wipe out your church, your finances, your reputation and your future. Trifling with disloyalty can cost you everything.

11. The spirit of heaviness operates in those who leave in rebellion.

To appoint unto them that mourn in Zion, to give unto them beauty for ashes, the oil of joy for mourning, the

garment of praise for THE SPIRIT OF HEAVINESS; that they might be called trees of righteousness, the planting of the Lord, that he might be glorified.

Isaiah 61:3

There is such a thing as the *spirit of heaviness*. The spirit of heaviness is the spirit of depression. When people are depressed they are enveloped in deep and negative thoughts. Their mood is depressed and they have thoughts that tend towards hopelessness. I have known several people who failed to share the dark thoughts and questions in their hearts. These dark and negative thoughts eventually led them to leave me even though I loved them dearly.

Without asking the necessary questions or communicating properly, they resigned and left what was valuable to them. Sometimes these depressed people do not even bother to resign.

People with a melancholic temperament tend to be subject to this demon. Depression is a powerful spirit and can lead people to commit suicide. Equally, when people have a spirit of depression, they can commit spiritual and ministry suicide. In one stroke, people who are depressed and filled with negative thoughts can take decisions that destroy their ministry.

I am sure you can see the similarities between physical suicide, spiritual suicide and ministerial suicide.

CHAPTER 3

The Unvoiced Messages of Those Who Leave You

Your lives are a letter written in our hearts, and EVERYONE CAN READ IT...

2 Corinthians 3:2 (NLT)

1. People who leave you give out many unvoiced messages.

> Your lives are a letter written in our hearts, and EVERYONE CAN READ IT and recognize our good work among you. Clearly, you are a letter from Christ prepared by us. IT IS WRITTEN NOT WITH PEN AND INK, but with the Spirit of the living God. It is carved not on stone, but on human hearts.
>
> 2 Corinthians 3:2-3 (NLT)

The "leavers" should not bother to claim innocence when people have bad thoughts about their former churches. Their lives and actions are letters that can be read. Paul, speaking of these "letters", said, "They are not written with pen and ink, but with the Spirit of the living God."

Paul said everyone could read these messages that are spoken without words.

You see, every action carries with it an unvoiced but distinct message. The message that is given by those who leave is often not written with pen and ink. *It is a message spoken without words.* People who leave, give off an unmistakable message! Whether they like it or not, everyone can read it, everyone can see it and everyone can feel it.

People who leave, love to hide behind the fact that they have not given any official reason for leaving. They say the Holy Spirit just spoke to them. They speak of long-standing visions that the Lord gave them. They claim to have said nothing evil and to have no malicious intentions for leaving. But there are often many reasons why people walk away from someone they have been with for many years.

Most of the time, those who leave you claim that God has led them to do so. But this is often a convenient smokescreen that they can hide behind to prevent further questions. So why is the departure of people such a painful experience?

Why is the departure of a leader or a long-standing associate not something that passes unnoticed? Why does it leave a lingering and bitter taste in our mouths?

The answer is simple: People who leave you do not leave quietly. They leave a message for all to ponder over. This message is usually destructive in its effect!

It pollutes and destroys the people that have been left behind and helps the *"departee"* to gain a following.

Most of the people who depart claim to have heard from God and officially give no other reason for what they are doing. However, as time goes by, you hear snippets of things they have said. These comments make up the true reasons for their leaving.

2. People who leave you always give an official reason for leaving.

3. People who leave you also give unofficial hints as to why they left.

Through casual comments, conversations unguarded remarks, writings, texts, letters and emails, people who leave reveal why they really left. Through the informal grapevine, you will gradually piece together the mind of the "departee".

You may find out that he was actually angry or bitter about something. You may find out that he had always intended to break away. He may say he had only intended to work in the ministry for five years. You may find out that these people are after money and independence.

It is so sad that the Holy Spirit is the one who has to take the blame for all their actions. People who leave always say the Holy Spirit is leading them. You can deceive some of the people some of the time but you cannot deceive all the people all the time. Eventually the true motives for people's actions are exposed.

4. The most painful part of the message of people who leave you are the questions they generate.

Those who leave you generate questions about everything. These questions often go unanswered and give rise to rumours. Many questions about your character, your integrity, your leadership and your wisdom are released into the atmosphere by the departure of one person.

These painful questions do not have ready answers and lead to suggestions and allegations about your character. People are forced to conjure up reasons to explain why they had to leave. The "departees" are asked many questions:

"Why did you have to leave?

What happened?

Was there a problem?

What is going on?

What's happening in your camp?"

People are shocked and surprised when someone leaves!

The "departee" smiles smugly and gives a vague answer. He knows that people are going to start thinking about reasons why somebody like him should walk away from the church. And that is exactly what he wants them to do! He is hopeful that people will eventually arrive at certain conclusions which he wants them to have.

I want you to understand the implied but unspoken messages of the people who leave you. When you understand what they are trying to do, it will help you to combat them in the spirit and overcome the onslaught of demonic attacks against your mind. Through this chapter you will fortify yourself against the attacks of the devil that come against you when people leave you.

5. People who leave you send the same messages that Jeroboam gave to Israel.

The story of Jeroboam's departure presents us with the quintessential departee who typifies all the characteristics of someone who leaves you and rebels against your authority.

Rehoboam and Jeroboam have similar sounding names. Many people do not know or remember the difference between these gentlemen. If you remember the letter "R" for "rightful" it will help you to remember that Rehoboam was the rightful heir to the throne of Solomon. However, Jeroboam who had worked as a servant to King Solomon rebelled against Rehoboam and broke away with ten of the twelve tribes of Israel.

God allowed this to happen because of the mistakes of Solomon. Ten out of the twelve members of Rehoboam's kingdom were lost through the actions of Jeroboam. God allowed this terrible experience to happen to Rehoboam because of Solomon's mistake. Even though the Lord allowed Jeroboam to succeed it presents us with a vivid illustration of how "departees" behave and the messages they leave in their wake.

God allowed Judas to betray the Lord and bring about the will of God through the cross. But the story of Judas teaches us valuable lessons about traitors and disloyalty. Similarly, God allowed Jeroboam to break away from Rehoboam and reduce his kingdom (church) by eighty per cent or more.

Even though the Lord allowed it, we can also learn valuable lessons about how "departees" and rebels operate. This will help all leaders to mature and combat the scourge of proud and wicked men who rise up to scatter His church. The Lord prophesied that upon His departure grievous wolves would enter the flock to scatter it. Jeroboam scattered the flock of Israel and it has never been the same again.

Every good shepherd must rise up and learn how to combat the spirit of Jeroboam and the spirit of Judas. Do not allow traitors to operate freely in your system. Do not allow the spirit of Jeroboam to operate in your church.

The spirit of Jeroboam is the spirit of rebellion! After the Lord used Jeroboam to bring about His will, He passed a very severe judgment on Jeroboam and His entire family. Jeroboam's entire family was wiped from the surface of the earth as a judgment against him.

It is only because Solomon disobeyed the Lord that the devil was given access to wreak havoc in Israel. Jeroboam was only the physical instrument for the onslaught of the devil on David and Solomon's kingdom.

6. People who leave send a message that there are alternatives to your church.

> Whereupon THE KING took counsel, and MADE TWO CALVES OF GOLD, and said unto them, it is too much for you to go up to Jerusalem: behold thy gods, O Israel, which brought thee up out of the land of Egypt.
>
> And HE SET THE ONE IN BETHEL, AND THE OTHER PUT HE IN DAN.
>
> And this thing became a sin: for the people went to worship before the one, even unto Dan.
>
> 1 Kings 12:28-30

Jeroboam, the classic "departee", established an alternative centre of worship for Israel. He made them think that there were alternatives to worshipping in Jerusalem. "Jerusalem is not the only place you can find God. You can also find God in *Dan* or in *Bethel*." This is often the message of the people who leave.

When a pastor sets up a church near a ministry he used to belong to, what message do you think he is giving? He is saying to all and sundry, "such and such" is not the only place where you can worship. There are alternatives to the church you've been attending. My new ministry is an alternative to that church. Why don't you try something new? You will discover a new experience of worship under my new leadership. You will be surprised to find that you can have everything that you had in the old place and more in my new alternative ministry."

This is the unspoken but implied message of the multitudes of pastors who leave churches in anger and rebellion. They say, "I will teach you a lesson. I will show the whole world that there are alternatives to your ministry. We don't all have to attend that man's church. They destabilize the committed members by giving them other options. This message scatters the congregation and confuses them.

I have had associate pastors who have left me and started churches a short distance away. Why do you think they started these churches so near their former home? They wanted the very people who attended my church to see their new church as an alternative place of worship.

7. People who leave you give a message that 'I am as good as you are.'

> And JEROBOAM ORDAINED A FEAST in the eighth month, on the fifteenth day of the month, LIKE UNTO THE FEAST THAT IS IN JUDAH, and he offered upon the altar...
>
> 1 Kings 12:32

Jeroboam organized programmes in Dan and Bethel that were just like the programmes in Jerusalem. The subtle message, "I'm as good as you are" comes out clearly from these actions. Once people get the message that "what is here is as good as what is there" they may have enough reasons to leave.

Although they will not admit it, most "leavers" are setting up alternatives to the place they came from and are saying, "What we have here is as good as what he has there."

I remember one breakaway pastor who promised he would not behave in this way. Before I realized he had actually started a church a short distance away from the church he had pastored for five years. Obviously, he was setting up an alternative to his former church. He was telling everyone, "You don't need to go there anymore. You can come here!"

Obviously, there were many gullible church members who saw the location of his new church as a convenient alternative. This rebellious pastor continued to add insult to injury by sending out personal invitations to my church members anytime he was having a programme. He used the addresses and mailing lists of the people he had pastored for five years to invite everyone to his new "alternative" church. Without saying those particular words he was presenting himself as an alternative and saying, "What I have here is as good as what they have there."

This is exactly what Jeroboam did. This is the spirit of Jeroboam at work! Jeroboam set up feasts in Dan and Bethel that could rival the feasts that were held in Jerusalem. Pastors with the spirit of Jeroboam set up their churches and say, "It is just like the feast in Judah!"

Dear pastor, you are dealing with the spirit of Jeroboam when you have to fight with people who set up camp a short distance from where they used to be.

8. People who leave send a message that you are a very bad person and it is a very difficult thing to stay under your leadership.

> And Rehoboam went to Shechem: for all Israel were come to Shechem to make him king.
>
> And it came to pass, when Jeroboam the son of Nebat, who was yet in Egypt, heard of it, (for he was fled from the presence of king Solomon, and Jeroboam dwelt in Egypt;)
>
> That they sent and called him. And Jeroboam and all the congregation of Israel came, and spake unto Rehoboam, saying,
>
> THY FATHER MADE OUR YOKE GRIEVOUS: NOW THEREFORE MAKE THOU THE GRIEVOUS SERVICE OF THY FATHER, AND HIS HEAVY YOKE WHICH HE PUT UPON US, LIGHTER, AND WE WILL SERVE THEE.
>
> And he said unto them, Depart yet for three days, then come again to me. And the people departed.
>
> 1 Kings 12:1-5

Jeroboam made it clear that it was a terrible experience to work under Solomon. He described working for Solomon as "grievous service". He said, "Your father made us suffer under a grievous burden. We cannot continue to live under these terrible and unbearable conditions." This is the message that people who leave want to transmit to the rest of the world. *"It was a difficult place to be! It was an intolerable and very difficult experience to belong to that team."*

Why would people leave if it wasn't unbearable? There must be some good reason for which they had to leave.

Whether they say it or not this message is alluded to by the "departees". This is why it is such an unpleasant experience to be abandoned, deserted or left by someone who has belonged to your team for many years. There is always a hint that you were a difficult person to be with that is why people had to leave.

Jeroboam is the best example of a person who leaves your team in the worst possible way.

Such people want the world to have bad feelings towards you. They want people to think and to know that being anywhere under any circumstance is better than being with you.

9. People who leave say it will be better to manage your own affairs than to be part of a team.

> So when all Israel saw that the king hearkened not unto them, the people answered the king, saying, what portion have we in David? Neither have we inheritance in the son of Jesse: to your tents, O Israel: now SEE TO THINE OWN HOUSE, David. So Israel departed unto their tents.
>
> 1 Kings 12:16

Many rebellious breakaway "departee" dissenters hold the view that it is always better to be on your own than to work for anyone else. It is true that it is a privilege to work without having a supervisor or a boss. But not everyone is called to be an independent leader. Most people are not called to be independent leaders. Most people are called to be part of a following of gifted independent leaders who are called into that special role.

To attempt to become something you are not called to be is one of the dangerous and demonic moves you could ever make. It is such decisions that lead to the many tragedies of ministry.

Remember that the first great example of religious "departees" was Satan himself. He moved out of his position and became the evil spirit that we know him to be. Since then, Satan has inspired many a person to do exactly what he did and to become exactly what he is today – a rebellious, worthless and withered branch. Indeed, such rebellious elements are worthy of nothing but eternal fire and damnation.

May you never follow this example into damnation! May you never be a bad example for others to follow!

10. People who leave allude to the fact that there are many sinister reasons for which they had to leave.

Rebellious and breakaway pastors leave everyone to imagine what exactly these dark sinister things could be.

When a woman walks away from her marriage to a well-known man of God, what is she saying?

She is saying to the rest of the world, "There are things you don't know about. It's not as it seems! There are many ugly, unpalatable secrets about this man which I alone know about. After all, I was married to him for several years. Who else would know better?"

Even though this may not be the truth it is the most believed story! The departure of a close aide always triggers the spread of stories. Whether it is the right story or not, a message is transmitted to the grapevine. Whether it is the truth or not, the actions of the "departee" transmit a message.

11. People who leave you send a message that it will be easier to follow them than to follow your old pastor.

> And Jeroboam said in his heart, now shall the kingdom return to the house of David:

> If this people go up to do sacrifice in the house of the Lord at Jerusalem, then shall the heart of this people turn again unto their lord, even unto Rehoboam king of Judah, and they shall kill me, and go again to Rehoboam king of Judah.
>
> Whereupon the king took counsel, and made two calves of gold, and said unto them, IT IS TOO MUCH FOR YOU TO GO UP TO JERUSALEM: behold thy gods, O Israel, which brought thee up out of the land of Egypt.
>
> And he set the one in Bethel, and the other put he in Dan.
>
> 1 Kings 12:26-29

"Departees" and leavers love to let people feel that it will be *easier* to be in *their* church. They describe their old church as a difficult place to belong to. They attract members by making it sound as though it will be much easier and simpler for them to belong to their new breakaway sect.

Of course this is a ploy used by desperados who are trying to build up something new. They need to look successful quickly to justify their leaving. In order to do this, they offer "incentives" to would-be followers.

Jeroboam, the classic anarchical rebel, exemplified this principle very well. He said to the people that it was too much for them to travel all the way to Jerusalem. He made them know that he had created a new place of worship that did not involve all the hassles of travelling to Jerusalem.

Many simple-minded people would be taken in by such incentives. But the deep and the mature are not deceived by the song of a liar and a sheep thief.

Many years ago, I met a pastor who had taken over an entire branch church of a denomination. He had renamed the church and informed the congregation that they were no longer belonging to the old denomination and that they were now a brand new church with a new name and a new founder.

I paid a casual visit to this traitorous fellow because he was an old acquaintance and I could not believe that he was doing such things. I asked him what exactly he was trying to achieve.

He explained, "We have a new church with a new name. We have a brand new vision and a brand new style of leadership."

I stared at him in disbelief as he continued to speak.

"In this church there will no more be authoritarian leadership. All of us will have a say."

He continued, "Also, in the old church only the senior pastor's message was important. But in this church all the assistant and associate pastors' messages will be important. We will produce the messages of all pastors and equally promote the CDs and DVDs of all the associate pastors."

He explained, "The senior pastor will not monopolize the pulpit any longer. All pastors will have the opportunity to preach."

Just like Jeroboam, this pastor was laying out his new exciting policies for the church. He wanted to have a church that was more attractive for associate pastors. He sought to attract people through his policies of plurality of ideas and a democratic shared leadership. Unfortunately, it was not long before his associates conspired against him and threw him out of the church.

12. People who leave you send a message that people should not give their money to your ministry.

> IF THIS PEOPLE GO UP TO DO SACRIFICE IN THE HOUSE OF THE LORD AT JERUSALEM, THEN SHALL THE HEART OF THIS PEOPLE TURN AGAIN UNTO THEIR LORD, even unto Rehoboam king of Judah, and they shall kill me, and go again to Rehoboam king of Judah.
>
> Whereupon the king took counsel, and made two calves of gold, and said unto them, It is too much for you to go up to

Jerusalem: behold thy gods, O Israel, which brought thee up out of the land of Egypt.

And he set the one in Bethel, and the other put he in Dan.

1 Kings 12:27-29

Since money is one of the common reasons why people leave you, it is no surprise that they try to re-direct the finances of your loyal followers to themselves. Jeroboam, the archetypal "departee" fervently sought to prevent the offerings and sacrifices from going to Jerusalem. He wanted them to be brought to where he was lest the hearts of the people turned back to their real leader.

Some years ago, I had a church with a few members. Out of these few members, I had about five or six prominent, well to do people. One day, one of my leading pastors decided to leave and set up an alternative place of worship a few metres from where we were. I was shocked at his move. But it was nothing new because Jeroboam's history had been written thousands of years before he existed. Jeroboam set up his new ministry in Dan and Bethel. But this fellow set up camp a few metres away. And there was more to come.

I found out that this "leaver" had spoken to many of my prominent and well to do members, inviting them to be part of his new ministry. I was aghast as I realised that he was attempting to take with him my chief supporters.

But this was not a new move. It was an old move recorded thousands of years ago in the history of the Jewish kings.

When the spirit of Jeroboam attacks your ministry it deals a blow against your offerings and your sacrifices. These people can ruin entire churches and cripple thriving ministries. That is why you must not joke with them nor treat them lightly.

The Successful Pastor

Your ministry can grind to a halt through the activities of a Jeroboam in your midst. One day, one of my pastors began a church in a remote part of Europe. Being a black man, he was excited because it seemed that even white people were interested in his ministry. I began getting weekly exciting reports about this successful pastor's exploits. From five they grew to ten, twenty and then over one hundred and fifty. This brother was one excited and successful pastor!

One day, I asked him, "Who are all the white people in your church. Where do they come from?"

He told me, "Amazingly, they are all from a particular country in Eastern Europe."

"Wow," I said, "That is exciting."

But as we were celebrating the great growth of this church the spirit of Jeroboam was gaining a foothold in the church.

The choir leader was a strong charismatic personality just like Jeroboam and he began to draw the hearts of the people away from their pastor.

One day, the successful pastor called and told us that a great tragedy had happened. The charismatic choir leader, with the spirit of Jeroboam, had led the entire congregation away and started a new alternative church.

In one day, the successful pastor lost almost every single member of the congregation. This large growing church with one hundred and fifty members shrank to less than five members in a day. He lost everything through the powerful move of a man anointed with the spirit of Jeroboam. That is why you must not look lightly upon the presence of independent-minded people. The independent and separatist mind is a dangerous killer cancer to the body.

Dear friend, I urge you to take this subject of loyalty and disloyalty very seriously. Your entire ministry can be destroyed if you do not deal decisively with disloyal people.

13. People who leave you appoint unqualified people into positions of authority.

> Whereupon the king took counsel, and made two calves of gold, and said unto them, It is too much for you to go up to Jerusalem: behold thy gods, O Israel, which brought thee up out of the land of Egypt.
>
> And he set the one in Bethel, and the other put he in Dan.
>
> And this thing became a sin: for the people went to worship before the one, even unto Dan.
>
> And he made an house of high places, AND MADE PRIESTS OF THE LOWEST OF THE PEOPLE, which were not of the sons of Levi.
>
> 1 Kings 12:28-31

This is another characteristic of desperate rebellious leaders who break away and steal sections of the congregation. They are clouds without water, twice dead and foaming at the mouth because they have destroyed the flocks of the Lord.

Eleven New Pastors

One day, I had a pastor who broke away from our church. He wrote a short letter to me stating he had decided to leave our ministry. This pastor had had the time to influence the people and so was able to deceive and lead away about eighty percent of the congregation. He now had about fifty members to begin his new ministry.

The surprising part of this story came a few months later when I heard the rumour that this pastor had appointed eleven new pastors to be his associates. I wondered to myself, "How come he is suddenly ordaining eleven new pastors? Where are these people from? What training do they have? What calling do they have?"

But this is one of the typical moves of renegade ministers. They often do exactly what Jeroboam did, ordaining and appointing men of the lowest sort to occupy the high positions in the ministry. Of course, this makes nonsense of spiritual authority and confuses the flock.

But you may ask: "Why do they appoint such people into positions of authority?" Is that what they learnt from the places they just left? Often the answer is No!

Perhaps, they do this to appease the "opinion leaders" who supported their uprising and to give them a "reward for helping" in the conspiracy. But their end will be as disastrous as their leader's. They have welded themselves to a rebellious person.

Keep watching these rebels! Their end is one and the same!

14. People who leave you give a message that there is no need to go to great lengths to express your loyalty.

> Whereupon THE KING took counsel, and MADE TWO CALVES OF GOLD, and said unto them, IT IS TOO MUCH FOR YOU TO GO UP TO JERUSALEM: behold thy gods, O Israel, which brought thee up out of the land of Egypt.
>
> 1 Kings 12:28

One of the things these "departees" love to do is to prevent the pilgrimages that loyal people make to their home. Why bother to travel all the way there? There is no need for such an extreme show of loyalty.

One day, whilst in Tulsa, I heard Kenneth Hagin announcing a homecoming meeting for his Rhema graduates. The Holy Spirit dropped it into my heart that it was a good idea to have a homecoming for our pastors and churches. This is a concept which is practised by almost every religion, group or movement. Moslems have their Hajj pilgrimage and most denominations have a huge annual gathering of their congregations and ministers in a particular place.

These are events where loyalists who are scattered all over the world congregate and show their love and allegiance to the home that gave birth to all of them.

In the Jewish religion, the people of God would gather three times a year in Jerusalem for the feasts of Israel. They would worship the Lord and present their offerings of praise and worship. Notice how David describes the importance of a place to attend a homecoming programme.

> Our feet shall stand within thy gates, O Jerusalem. Jerusalem is builded as a city that is compact together: whither the tribes go up, the tribes of the Lord, unto the testimony of Israel, to give thanks unto the name of the Lord.
>
> Psalm 122:2-4

Even today, the Jews part with the saying, "Next year in Jerusalem."

It was this loyal gathering that Jeroboam was seeking to disrupt! He did not want people to travel any more to Jerusalem. He created "new churches" in Dan and Bethel and sent out the message that there was no need to travel all the way to Jerusalem any more. Going to Jerusalem was a silly, fruitless, expensive and old-fashioned thing to do.

When I introduced this "homecoming" idea, I quickly noticed the different responses which revealed different levels of loyalty. In particular, I remember a pastor who made an annual pilgrimage to *another* denomination's annual "homecoming" programme. It may not have been called a "homecoming" but it was. Instead of coming for *our* homecoming, he was attending the homecoming of another denomination every year.

Obviously, there was something questionable about his loyalty. It was only a matter of time before this person fully expressed his disloyalty by breaking away completely.

CHAPTER 4

The Accusations of Those Who Leave You

1. ZACCHAEUS ACCUSED PEOPLE IN ORDER TO TAKE AWAY THEIR POSSESSIONS.

> And when Jesus came to the place, he looked up, and saw him, and said unto him, Zacchaeus, make haste, and come down; for to day I must abide at thy house.
>
> And he made haste, and came down, and received him joyfully.
>
> And when they saw it, they all murmured, saying, that he was gone to be guest with a man that is a sinner.
>
> And Zacchaeus stood, and said unto the Lord; Behold, Lord, the half of my goods I give to the poor; AND IF I HAVE TAKEN ANY THING FROM ANY MAN BY FALSE ACCUSATION, I restore him fourfold.
>
> And Jesus said unto him, This day is salvation come to this house, forsomuch as he also is a son of Abraham.
>
> Luke 19:5-9

2. MINISTERS OF THE GOSPEL ARE ACCUSED IN ORDER TO TAKE AWAY THEIR MEMBERS.

When Zacchaeus repented he gave himself away and let the whole world know what he had been up to. The confessions of Zacchaeus are a revelation about the purpose and powerful effect of accusations.

Zacchaeus revealed that he had been accusing people, telling lies about them to take things from them. Notice his words, *"If I have taken any thing from any man by false accusation..."*. He took things away from people by falsely accusing them. Perhaps he would accuse one of evading tax and based on that he would seize the person's goods. He would accuse another of getting his contract in the wrong way and through that he would take away their contracts.

Systematically, through false accusation and intimidation, he took away the wealth and possessions of many people. This is why ministers of the Gospel are accused of different things – in order to take away their members.

Ministers are accused of immorality because it is a good reason for people to leave their folds and desert them.

Ministers are accused of immorality so that people do not stay with them any longer. Why would you want to stay with an immoral person?

Ministers are accused of misappropriating money so that people lose confidence in them and leave them. Why should you have a thief as a pastor?

Ministers are accused of homosexuality. Why should you follow a pastor who is a homosexual?

Ministers are accused of being racist so that people from other races will turn away from them.

Ministers are accused of being bad leaders. Why should you follow a bad leader?

3. MOSES WAS ACCUSED IN ORDER TO TAKE AWAY THE FOLLOWING HE HAD IN ISRAEL.

> Is it a small thing that thou hast brought us up out of a land that floweth with milk and honey, to kill us in the wilderness, except thou make thyself altogether a prince over us? Moreover thou hast not brought us into a land that floweth with milk and honey, or given us inheritance of fields and vineyards: wilt thou put out the eyes of these men? We will not come up.
>
> Numbers 16:13-14

People who leave you need to have a good reason to do what they do. Often, they do not have anything substantial to present as the reason for their actions. Because of this, they are forced to resort to accusations. They accuse you so that others will stop following you.

Moses' experience with Korah and his company will give you the reassurance that there is nothing new under the sun. If they could say those words to Moses then do not be surprised what may be said to you. Moses was accused of terrible things by Korah and his family. These accusations, if true, were more than enough to make everyone leave Moses. The following statements are commonly used by rebellious people who are looking for excuses to explain their actions. Amazingly, Moses experienced every single one of these accusations. Do not be surprised if you experience some of these yourself. It just shows that you are walking in the footsteps of great people.

i. You are exalting yourself above the rest of us. Moses was also accused of pride and self exaltation.

> And they gathered themselves together against Moses and against Aaron, and said unto them, ye take too much upon you, seeing all the congregation are holy, every one of them, and the lord is among them: WHEREFORE THEN LIFT YE UP YOURSELVES ABOVE THE CONGREGATION OF THE LORD?
>
> Numbers 16:3

ii. You are not special. You are not the only one who is called of God. Many people are called by God. Moses was accused of thinking he was the only righteous man.

By this statement, Moses was accused of the sin of glorifying himself. He was described as a self-centred egomaniac by Korah and his associates.

> And they gathered themselves together against Moses and against Aaron, and said unto them, ye take too much upon you, seeing ALL THE CONGREGATION ARE HOLY, EVERY ONE OF THEM, AND THE LORD IS AMONG THEM: wherefore then lift ye up yourselves above the congregation of the Lord?
>
> Numbers 16:3

iii. Why do you make yourself different? We will not come to your meeting. Moses was despised publicly by Dathan and Abiram.

> And MOSES SENT TO CALL DATHAN AND ABIRAM, the sons of Eliab: WHICH SAID, WE WILL NOT COME UP:
>
> Numbers 16:12

iv. You are not a good leader and you have not brought us to a good place. Moses was accused of not fulfilling his promises.

> Moreover THOU HAST NOT BROUGHT US INTO A LAND THAT FLOWETH WITH MILK AND HONEY, OR GIVEN US INHERITANCE OF FIELDS AND VINEYARDS: wilt thou put out the eyes of these men? We will not come up.
>
> Numbers 16:14

v. If we follow you, you will destroy us. Moses was accused of trying to kill the people.

> Is it a small thing that thou hast brought us up out of a land that floweth with milk and honey, TO KILL US IN

THE WILDERNESS, except thou make thyself altogether a prince over us?

Numbers 16:13

vi. We would have been better off if we had stayed at our old place. Moses was accused of leading the people to a worse situation.

Is it a small thing that THOU HAST BROUGHT US UP OUT OF A LAND THAT FLOWETH WITH MILK AND HONEY, to kill us in the wilderness, except thou make thyself altogether a prince over us?

Moreover THOU HAST NOT BROUGHT US INTO A LAND THAT FLOWETH WITH MILK AND HONEY, OR GIVEN US INHERITANCE OF FIELDS AND VINEYARDS: wilt thou put out the eyes of these men? We will not come up.

Numbers 16:13-14

vii. You want to be a "big man" and lord it over us. Moses was accused of trying to make himself a prince over Israel.

Is it a small thing that thou hast brought us up out of a land that floweth with milk and honey, to kill us in the wilderness, EXCEPT THOU MAKE THYSELF ALTOGETHER A PRINCE OVER US?

Numbers 16:13

viii. You want us to follow you blindly. Moses was accused of trying to blind the eyes of people.

Moreover thou hast not brought us into a land that floweth with milk and honey, or given us inheritance of fields and vineyards: WILT THOU PUT OUT THE EYES OF THESE MEN? We will not come up.

Numbers 16: 14

ix. You are enriching yourself through us. Moses was also accused of trying to enrich himself.

And Moses was very wroth, and said unto the Lord, Respect not thou their offering: I HAVE NOT TAKEN ONE ASS FROM THEM, neither have I hurt one of them.
Numbers 16:15

4. JESUS CHRIST WAS ACCUSED IN ORDER TO TAKE AWAY HIS LIFE.

When Satan wants to take away your life and ministry he will send people to accuse you of serious crimes, hoping to convince people to do away with you. When the Chief priests and elders desired to kill Jesus Christ, they began to accuse him of preposterous things that He had never done.

And the whole multitude of them arose, and led him unto Pilate. And they began to ACCUSE HIM, saying, we found this fellow perverting the nation, and forbidding to give tribute to Caesar, saying that he himself is Christ a King.

And Pilate asked him, saying, Art thou the King of the Jews? And he answered him and said, Thou sayest it.

Then said Pilate to the chief priests and to the people, I find no fault in this man.

And they were the more fierce, saying, HE STIRRETH UP THE PEOPLE, teaching throughout all Jewry, beginning from Galilee to this place.

Then he QUESTIONED WITH HIM IN MANY WORDS; but he answered him nothing.

And the chief priests and scribes stood and VEHEMENTLY ACCUSED him.

And Herod with his men of war set him at nought, and mocked him, and arrayed him in a gorgeous robe, and sent him again to Pilate.

And the same day Pilate and Herod were made friends together: for before they were at enmity between themselves.

Luke 23: 1-5, 9-12

They had one aim: to take away His life and end His ministry on the earth. Satan's principal weapon was the weapon of accusation. Numerous accusations were levelled against Jesus because they wanted to give Pilate enough reason to end His life and ministry on earth. But somehow, all these accusations did not make sense to Pilate.

5. THEY LEFT ME AND THEY ACCUSED ME.

Over the years, I have suffered many different kinds of accusations. These different accusations were intended to take away my members and my following. Very few pastors who left me did so quietly. Many of them walked out breathing different threats and accusations. I want to share with you some of these accusations because you will have your own share of accusations in the ministry. Every minister is accused of many things and you must get used to this kind of thing.

i. Those who left accused me of forcing people to listen to my preaching instead of allowing them to pray to the Holy Spirit for guidance on what to preach.

A rebellious pastor left my church claiming that ministers in our church could not follow the Holy Spirit. They claimed they had to listen to me instead of listening to God.

Of course, who would want to be in a church where the pastor does not hear from God? Who wants to be in a church where the Holy Spirit is not freely guiding and leading affairs?

I Believe My Pastors Should Listen to Messages I Have Preached

I teach my disciples to listen to messages I have preached for several reasons. Many of these reasons are solidly based on the

Scriptures and also on common sense. Rebellious men who want to leave should just leave without bothering to attack things they don't understand.

Please note some of the scriptural reasons for asking my pastors to listen to and learn from my messages and to preach from my books as well. I would recommend this to anyone who wants to do well in the ministry.

There is a clever accusation that seeks to ridicule this spiritually beautiful exercise of listening to messages of their leader.

Why You Should Listen to the Messages of Your Leader

1. I encourage pastors to listen to my messages in order to learn how to preach. "That ye be not slothful, but followers of them who through faith and patience inherit the promises" (Hebrews 6:12).

2. Listen to messages as a resource material that you can use to give you stuff to preach. Pastors have to preach many messages all the time and it is always a blessing to have a resource. The preaching and teaching messages of other ministers have been my greatest blessing and a source of inspiration.

3. Listen to messages because Paul asked Timothy to listen to his messages and repeat them. Read it for yourself: "Thou therefore, my son, be strong in the grace that is in Christ Jesus. And the things that thou hast heard of me among many witnesses, the same commit thou to faithful men, who shall be able to teach others also" (2 Timothy 2:1-2).

4. I encourage pastors to listen to messages in order to catch the anointing. Notice how the Holy Spirit fell on people who were listening to Peter preaching (Acts 10:44).

5. I encourage pastors to listen to messages because there are different callings. The apostle will hear directly from God but the pastors under the apostle may receive a lot of direction through the apostle. Read it for yourself. It is all over the Bible. Paul described himself as an apostle who had seen Jesus Christ. These are heavyweight credentials. "Am I not an apostle? Am I not free? Have I not seen Jesus Christ our Lord? Are not ye my work in the Lord?" (1 Corinthians 9:1). He gave a lot of instructions to Timothy and Titus. He even asked them to read his letters and books to the congregation. Even though Titus and Timothy had the Holy Spirit, Paul told them many things to say and to do.

TO TIMOTHY, my dearly beloved son: Grace, mercy, and peace, from God the Father and Christ Jesus our Lord.

Hold fast the form of sound words, which thou hast heard of me, in faith and love which is in Christ Jesus.

That good thing which was committed unto thee keep by the Holy Ghost which dwelleth in us.

2 Timothy 1:2, 13-14

TO TITUS, mine own son after the common faith: Grace, mercy, and peace, from God the Father and the Lord Jesus Christ our Saviour.

For this cause left I thee in Crete, that thou shouldest set in order the things that are wanting, and ordain elders in every city, as I had appointed thee:

Titus 1:4-5

But speak thou the things which become sound doctrine:

That the aged men be sober, grave, temperate, sound in faith, in charity, in patience.

The aged women likewise, that they be in behaviour as becometh holiness, not false accusers, not given to much wine, teachers of good things;

That they may teach the young women to be sober, to love their husbands, to love their children,

To be discreet, chaste, keepers at home, good, obedient to their own husbands, that the word of God be not blasphemed.

Young men likewise exhort to be sober minded.

In all things shewing thyself a pattern of good works: in doctrine shewing uncorruptness, gravity, sincerity,

Sound speech, that cannot be condemned; that he that is of the contrary part may be ashamed, having no evil thing to say of you.

Exhort servants to be obedient unto their own masters, and to please them well in all things; not answering again;

Not purloining, but shewing all good fidelity; that they may adorn the doctrine of God our Saviour in all things.

Titus 2:1-10

ii. Those who left accused me of forcing people to preach from my books instead of allowing them to pray to the Holy Spirit for guidance.

These rebellious men make derogatory comments about my pastors preaching from books that I have written.

Why do they accuse me in this way? Why do people try to ridicule me? They accuse me because they want people to leave me. They want my congregation to forsake me. They want people to stop coming to my church. Like Zacchaeus they want to deprive me of my members!

But Paul asked for his letters to be read. Paul's letters were Paul's books.

Don't we call them the book of Corinthians or the book of Ephesians?

Don't we call them the books of the Bible?

Why do men inspired by evil spirits criticize holy practices like listening to messages? The answer is simple. Like Zacchaeus who took away the valuable possessions of many people, they want to take away our people! They want to take away our following! They want to take away our loyal members! Notice the Scriptures below and how Paul asked for his books to be read to the churches.

> **I CHARGE YOU by the Lord THAT THIS EPISTLE BE READ UNTO ALL the holy brethren.**
>
> **1 Thessalonians 5:27**

> **Salute the brethren which are in Laodicea, and Nymphas, and the church which is in his house.**
> **And WHEN THIS EPISTLE IS READ AMONG YOU, CAUSE THAT IT BE READ ALSO IN THE CHURCH OF THE LAODICEANS; and that ye likewise read the *epistle* from Laodicea.**
>
> **Colossians 4:15-16**

iii. Those who left accused me of producing clones instead of real ministers.

Some people have tried to re-describe the beautiful principle of discipleship. They insult my pastors – describing them as 'clones'. By this, they are saying that my pastors are mindless robots who cannot think for themselves but simply copy what they do not understand.

Why do people speak like this? Why do wicked men rise up to portray good things as evil? These wicked men have the stealing spirit of unconverted Zacchaeus. Some people speak against copying and following mentors, saying that we must follow the example of David who was an original and refused to use Saul's armour.

But these clever sayings go against the words of Jesus. Jesus said it was a good thing when disciples were just like their masters. "It is enough for the disciple that he be as his master, and the servant as his lord... " (Matthew10:25).

Indeed, the goal of the disciple is to be just like his master.

Even the history of mankind has shown that emulation is the key to the spread of prosperity. And yet these "empty clouds filled with hatred" speak evil of what they do not understand.

iv. Those who left accused me of wanting to reap where I had not sown.

"And the one also who had received the one talent came up and said, 'Master, I knew you to be a hard man, REAPING WHERE YOU DID NOT SOW, AND gathering where you scattered no seed" (Matthew 25:24-25 (NASB)

And yet I have sown much prayer and fasting into the churches. I have given my life to preach the Word of God through tapes, CDs, DVDs, conventions, camps and services. I have done things that have benefitted many fledgling churches. How can you say I want to reap where I have not sown?

I have sown many journeys; I have sown missionaries and pastors into the nations.

I have sown by suffering false accusations; I have sown by being dishonoured; I have sown by being in hunger; and enduring evil reports.

I have sown by suffering different crises and dark days in my ministry. I have sown seeds by suffering distresses and discouragement.

I have sown by sacrificing my children's education;

I have sown by being in dangerous situations like accidents, being attacked by armed robbers, by being mocked and derided.

v. Those who left accused me of being an exacting man.

Every language has a phrase describing good leaders in exactly the same way. In the Ga language of Ghana, such a person is described as *"e sane wa waa dientse"*. In the Fante language of Ghana he is described as *"n'asem ye dzen"*. In the

Yoruba language of Nigeria such a person is described thus: *"o ti le ju"*.

When I checked out what these meant in English I realised that most good leaders were accused of being exacting leaders. Jesus gave Himself as an example of the master who went on a long journey leaving some talents with different servants. In the end, the master was accused of being exacting! But good leaders are often accused of being exacting! I was amazed when I found out what it really means to be exacting.

If you describe a person as exacting you mean that he is taxing, difficult, gruelling, hard, overbearing, high-handed, unsparing, harsh, strict, cruel, brutal, stern, relentless, rigid, stringent, rigorous, unyielding, uncompromising, unreasonable, merciless, inflexible, pitiless, fussy, fastidious and difficult to please.

But why do people accuse good leaders of being difficult to please? They are trying to take you away from where you belong. They are trying to steal your members; that is why you are being accused of so many nasty-sounding things.

If someone describes you as being exacting just remember that all good leaders, including our Lord Jesus, would be accused of being exacting. "And another came, saying, 'Master, behold your mina, which I kept put away in a handkerchief; for I was afraid of you, because you are AN EXACTING MAN; you take up what you did not lay down, and reap what you did not sow.'" Luke 19:20, 21 (NASB).

vi. Those who left accused me of building an empire.

But why would any one think of accusing me of this? Because they want to present me as an empire-building egomaniac who does not care about the Body of Christ. Who would want to follow somebody like that? I wouldn't. But this is a fantastic accusation because I spend so much time preaching in non-Lighthouse churches.

I hope you understand why Zacchaeus accused people falsely in order to take their treasures and why rebellious pastors accuse the churches they are leaving in order to take their treasured members.

vii. Those who left accused me of creating a cult because our church emphasizes loyalty.

How can I not place emphasis on loyalty and faithfulness when it is a subject that is mentioned over one hundred times in the Bible? The final judgment will be about two things: goodness and faithfulness.

Why would people accuse me of something like this? They accuse me because they want to take away my members. They want to frighten people away from me! It is a clever accusation because a cult is a scary thing to belong to. When you belong to a cult you cannot easily leave it. People whose hearts and mouths are filled with accusation will bow their knees and confess their sins when they meet Jesus. Ask Zacchaeus what happened to him and how he had to restore four-fold what he had stolen.

CHAPTER 5

How Those Who Leave You Set a Bad Example

For I gave you an example THAT YOU ALSO SHOULD DO AS I DID to you.

John 13:15 (NASB)

The message that we all give by our actions is: "Follow my example." Jesus Christ set an example intending us to do likewise. Whenever an example is set, it causes those who see it to copy it. This effect may be slow but it surely does happen over time.

Rebels and "leavers" are no exception to this law of example setting. Every time a leader or a prominent person leaves a church he issues an unspoken message to all and sundry. He says with his actions, *"Follow me, this is the right thing to do."*

That is why you must detect and resist disloyal people. You must fight them because they will destroy your church without speaking a word. By their actions alone, they shout out to the whole world and influence many people.

By their actions, they tell people, "Let's break this church down. Let's split it up. Let everyone know that they can do well without belonging to that group." Every rebel has that effect and every good pastor must learn how to cut back on the influence that "leavers" have. This is one reason why we must mark and avoid disloyal people (Romans 16:17). We must mention their names and warn our sheep about their bad influence.

The Evil Domino Spirit

The term "domino effect" is often used to describe a falling row of dominoes. The classic demonstration of the domino effect involves the setting up of a chain of dominoes and toppling the first domino. That domino topples the one next to it, and so on. In the end the long chain of dominoes will all come down. This domino effect happens because the energy required to topple the next domino is very small so the chain of toppling dominoes is self-sustaining.

Although the term domino effect is observed literally when there is a series of actual dominoes, this term is also used to describe a sequence of changes that occur in our world. The domino effect is seen in wars, governments, politics and even the church.

This linkage between events leading to wars, changes in government, changes in politics and changes in the church world is real. Indeed, the domino effect or the domino spirit is also felt in the church world.

When someone releases a domino sprit, what he does is repeated over and over again by others.

1. Jeroboam Releases a Domino Spirit

Jeroboam set the example with his act of rebellion against the legitimate heir to the throne of Solomon. Several other kings eventually emulated this action. These kings learnt the skills of rebellion from Jeroboam. They followed his example and did even worse things than Jeroboam. Jeroboam released a domino spirit of rebellion against authority.

> So when all Israel saw that the king hearkened not unto them, the people answered the king, saying, what portion have we in David? Neither have we inheritance in the son of Jesse: to your tents, O Israel: now see to thine own house, David. So Israel departed unto their tents.
>
> But as for the children of Israel which dwelt in the cities of Judah, Rehoboam reigned over them.
>
> Then king Rehoboam sent Adoram, who was over the tribute; and all Israel stoned him with stones, that he died. Therefore king Rehoboam made speed to get him up to his chariot, to flee to Jerusalem. So Israel rebelled against the house of David unto this day.
>
> And it came to pass, when all Israel heard that Jeroboam was come again, that they sent and called him unto the congregation, and made him king over all Israel: there was none that followed the house of David, but the tribe of Judah only.
>
> 1 Kings 12:16-20

2. Baasha Follows Jeroboam's Example

King Baasha was the first to follow the example of Jeroboam. He rose up against the son of Jeroboam and murdered him along with the family of Jeroboam. Where do you think king Baasha got the inspiration from? Where did the idea to rebel against a legitimate king come from?

> And Baasha the son of Ahijah, of the house of Issachar, conspired against him; and Baasha smote him at Gibbethon, which belonged to the Philistines; for Nadab and all Israel laid siege to Gibbethon.
>
> Even in the third year of Asa king of Judah did Baasha slay him, and reigned in his stead.
>
> And it came to pass, when he reigned, that he smote all the house of Jeroboam; he left not to Jeroboam any that breathed, until he had destroyed him, according unto the saying of the Lord, which he spake by his servant Ahijah the Shilonite:
>
> 1 Kings 15:27-29

3. Zimri Continues the Rebellion

King Zimri was the second king to follow Jeroboam's example. He also rebelled against the king of the day and murdered his entire household. Where do you think people get these ideas from? Obviously, he had learnt it from somewhere! Jeroboam was the great example setter in these things.

> And HIS SERVANT ZIMRI, captain of half his chariots, CONSPIRED AGAINST HIM, as he was in Tirzah, drinking himself drunk in the house of Arza steward of his house in Tirzah.
>
> And Zimri WENT IN AND SMOTE HIM, AND KILLED HIM, in the twenty and seventh year of Asa king of Judah, and reigned in his stead.
>
> And it came to pass, when he began to reign, as soon as he sat on his throne, that he slew all the house of Baasha: he

left him not one that pisseth against a wall, neither of his kinsfolks, nor of his friends.

1 Kings 16:9-11

The example-setting power of any action is seen throughout history. One event in one country leads to similar events in other countries.

When one event causes a similar event that in turn leads to another event, you have a full domino effect. An evil domino spirit is released into your ministry when one pastor's departure causes the departure of a series of other pastors.

Disloyalty and treachery can easily release an evil domino spirit into your church and ministry.

The Evil Domino Spirit: Number One Sets the Example

I once experienced the effect of the presence of an *evil domino spirit* of disloyalty through the actions of a pilot whom I had raised up to become a pastor.

Because he was a Boeing 747 pilot he was based in a large and wealthy city that was a hub for the airline he worked with. In spite of his high-up position as a 747 pilot he was a humble church member and we trained him to become a pastor. In spite of his frequent flights he was able to handle the church successfully and it grew nicely.

Everything worked out well until this pastor decided to break away and start a separate and independent ministry. An independent spirit took over and this gentleman did not want to be under supervision any longer.

But the real trouble this gentleman would inspire was yet to come. In spite of persistent warnings not to do so, he began his own new church near the one he used to be in charge of.

A few years later, people began to follow his example. Several members of the team of pastors to which he had belonged began to break away just as he had done some years earlier. They had learned from his example and were following suit.

One after the other they left the church and did exactly what they had seen him do. They all started splinter churches in and around their original churches. Soon, the horizon of the city was dotted with several splinter churches and hundreds of confused church members who did not know which little group to belong to.

Our church had been very stable before the epoch of this independent-spirited example-setting breakaway "departee" pilot pastor. A domino spirit of rebellion was released into the team of pastors through the actions of this first breakaway pastor. They had seen him break away and he seemed to have gotten away with it. They said to themselves, "If he can do that we can do that too."

There is nothing wrong with starting your own ministry. But there is something wrong when you set up yourself as an alternative to the congregation that you used to pastor thereby destroying it.

The evidence of the destructive effect of these actions is seen in the number of people that move from the main congregation to the breakaway's church, thereby subtly destroying the old congregation. You build up one congregation but you subtly destroy another.

We Know You by Your Fruits

You are known by your fruits and not by your words. You may claim to have a good attitude and be fighting for peace. But if your fruit is division, disloyalty and the subtle destruction of somebody else's ministry, it tells us who you are. If you are a son who rises up to bring confusion, division and dishonour to your father's house that tells us who you are!

There was a time that I had twenty-nine pastors in that city alone. No one had ever been disloyal or unfaithful towards me. They loved me very much and were thankful for the honour of being made pastors. They were grateful for the opportunity to serve the Lord in that town. The pastors themselves had never imagined that they would be honoured and ordained as pastors. But through the church they had been elevated and honoured in the ministry. I was personally close to many of them and had even hosted some of them in my own home before.

But with the advent of this pastor's breakaway, a new idea was released into the minds of other pastors. They began to follow the example of the 747 pilot whom I would like to call Number One.

The Evil Domino Spirit: Numbers Two and Three

Shortly after the pilot pastor's move to separate, another pastor decided to follow his bad example. I shall call this new breakaway pastor Number Two. Number Two decided to break away shortly after he had been appointed as a pastor. He took off with as many people as he could. But we quickly dispatched another pastor to stabilise the situation in that branch church. This stabilising pastor is the person I will call Number Three. Now, it happened that both Number Two and Number Three were medical doctors and worked in the same hospital. We sent Number Three with twelve families from the main church to stabilise and build up the congregation.

In our naiveté we never thought Number Three could turn against us. To our surprise, Number Three followed the example of Number One and Number Two. The conspiracy of Number Three was stronger and he successfully nabbed most of the church members. This was a great act of wickedness by Number Three.

He had conspired for a long time and stolen the hearts of the people. Indeed, the Lord will judge between us. After the wickedness of Number Three, there was nothing left of the church and we decided to completely close down our operations there.

The Evil Domino Spirit: Number Four

Then came Number Four, Number Five, Number Six and Number Seven. These four wrote to me indicating their unhappiness with the conditions under which they worked. These four pastors were friends because they happened to be in Law School together and had graduated as lawyers on the same day. Being lawyers, it was natural for them to give me an ultimatum. In their letter, they had warned me that if I did not comply they would decide on "the next step." "The next step" of course was their full and open rebellion. Thinking I could save the situation, I decided to comply with their ultimatum and granted their requests.

But Number Four did not wait to receive my reply. He checked out of the ministry before he could even read my response.

The Evil Domino Spirit: Number Five

Number Five, however, was happy with my response to their letter. He declared that he would continue to be a staunch and committed pastor of the ministry. He also affirmed his continued loyalty to me.

But as the crisis deepened, much confusion arose in the branch church that Number Five was pastoring. In the end, we decided to close it down and ask the members of this branch church to join the main church. But the whole church (whose hearts had been stolen by Number Five) revolted against me and formed a splinter church. Number Five lamented that he had become the unwilling leader of this separatist group.

The Evil Domino Spirit: Numbers Six and Seven

Numbers Six and Seven did receive my response and knew that I had complied with their ultimatum. In spite of that they decided that they would leave. This only showed that they had made up their minds anyway. Numbers Six and Seven proceeded to immediately form a new church in this same city. Now we had several splinter churches in one city.

The Evil Domino Spirit: Number Eight

Enter Number Eight. After number one to seven had fully manifested, Number Eight made a phone call to a senior pastor and told him that he was praying about leaving the church. He actually wanted this senior pastor to advise him on what to do. At a meeting, I confronted Number Eight about his intentions to leave and start another splinter church. I said to him, "Do whatever you want to do now." I told him that I knew that he was seeking advice on breaking away. He denied vehemently that he had any intentions of leaving and accused the senior pastor of lying. A few days later however, Number Eight did exactly what he had said he had no intentions of doing. Number Eight promptly proceeded to set up yet another church in the city.

As you can see, Number One set the example that released an evil domino spirit of rebellion. Number One did not just release a spirit of rebellion but he released a *domino* spirit of rebellion. A domino spirit has a different effect because it causes a cascade of chain reactions.

You need to understand the effect of the evil domino spirit to be fully motivated in your crusade against disloyalty and treachery.

The domino effect is the reason why countries in the same region have similar characteristics. They copy each other and learn from each other.

The domino effect is the effect of the presence of a "domino spirit". It is a chain reaction that occurs when a small change causes a similar change nearby, which then will cause another similar change, and so on.

The Domino Spirit in the World

1. The domino spirit caused Revolutions to take place around the world.

A revolution in one country often sparked off revolutions in other countries. You will notice the domino effect of world revolutions: The French revolution became a pattern for revolutions around the world. It has often been cited as an example of the way to have a revolution.

1. From 1775 to 1787, the North American Revolution took place. The French Revolution followed shortly after from 1789-1815.
2. From 1789 to 1815 the French Revolution took place.
3. From 1791 to 1804 the Haitian revolution took place and was greatly influenced by the French revolution.
4. From 1810-1825 the Spanish revolution took place, also inspired by earlier revolutions.

2. The domino spirit caused all African nations to fight for independence.

The fight for independence across the continent of Africa had this domino effect. The fight for independence in one country was often noticed by a neighbouring country. This stirred them up to fight for independence from their colonial masters. Soon, virtually all countries had their independence from colonial rule, whether they were ready for it or not.

1. 1951: Libya gained her independence.
2. 1952: Egypt gained her independence.
3. 1956: Sudan and Morocco gained independence.
4. 1957: Ghana (Gold Coast) was the first country south of the Sahara to gain independence.
5. 1958: Guinea also gained her independence.
6. 1960 : Algeria, Mauritania, Mali, Niger, Chad, Senegal, Sierra Leone, Cote d'Ivoire, Burkina Faso (Upper Volta), Togo, Benin (Dahomey), Nigeria, Cameroun, Gabon, Congo-Brazaville, Central African Republic, Congo-Leopoldville, Uganda, Kenya, Somalia, Rwanda, Burundi, Zambia, Malawi, Madagascar gained independence.
7. 1961: Tanganyika gained her independence.
8. 1963: Zanzibar gained her independence.

3. The domino spirit caused instability in West Africa.

When the evil domino spirit entered West Africa, it turned the entire sub-region into a wilderness. When an evil domino spirit enters a church or a denomination, it turns the entire church into a desolate ministry.

After African countries had gained independence, coup d'etats became the preferred style of rebellion. Once again, you will notice the domino effect of Coup d'états in the West Africa region in the late 1970's and early 80's. Within a span of five years several coups had taken place across several countries in the region introducing mostly leaders with no idea of how to rule a country.

All this history goes to prove why rebellion must be stopped dead in its tracks. It can have a devastating and spreading effect, destabilizing entire regions as people follow things they do not understand.

1. In 1978: Ghana - Fred Akuffo led a coup against Ignatius Kutu Acheampong.

2. In 1979: Ghana - Jerry John Rawlings led one against Hilla Limann.

3. In 1979: Equitorial Guinea - there was a coup staged by Teodoro Obiang Nguema Mbasogo.

4. In 1980: Guinea Bissau - João Bernardo Vieira toppled the government of Luis Cabral in a bloodless military coup on the 14th of November.

5. In 1980: Liberia - Staff Sergeant Samuel K Doe staged one against President William R. Tolbert, Jr and the Americo-Liberian elite.

6. In 1981: Ghana - there was yet another coup by Jerry John Rawlings against the government of President Hilla Limann.

7. In 1983: Burkina Faso - there was yet another coup by Blaise Compaoré against Jean-Baptiste Ouédraogo.

8. In 1984: Guinea - Lansana Conté also led a military coup against the government of the day.

4. The domino spirit caused Civil Wars in Africa.

Civil wars began to be fashionable in the West African region after Liberia showed the way to everyone. Gradually, the message was sinking through: "Arise O rebels and fight your governments". This is why it is important to prevent rebellions and breakaways. Every rebellion and breakaway leads to more rebellions and breakaways.

1. In 1989: Liberian civil war - the first Liberian Civil war was from 1989 to1996.

2. In 1990: Rwanda had a civil war which was a conflict within the Central African nation of Rwanda between the

government of President Juvénal Habyarimana and the rebel Rwandan Patriotic Front (RPF). The conflict began on 2 October 1990 when the RPF invaded and ostensibly ended on August 4, 1993 with the signing of the Arusha Accords to create a power-sharing government.

3. In 1991: The Sierra Leonean civil war began in 1991 and was officially declared over on 18 January 2002. Liberia ended up having two civil wars.
4. In 1993: Burundi had a civil war that lasted from 1993 to 2005.
5. In 1998: Congo embarked on a war that officially ended in 2003. It was the largest war in modern African history, it directly involved eight African nations, as well as about 25 armed groups. The Second Congo War, also known as Africa's World War and the Great War of Africa, began in August 1998 in the Democratic Republic of the Congo (formerly called Zaire), and officially ended in July 2003 when the Transitional Government of the Democratic Republic of the Congo took power (though hostilities continue to this day).
6. In 1999: Liberia embarked on a second civil war which lasted till 2003
7. In 2002: The Ivorian Civil War was a civil war in Côte d'Ivoire that began on September 19, 2002. Although most of the fighting ended by late 2004, the country remains split in two, with a rebel-held north and a government-held south.

5. The domino spirit caused the uprisings in the Arab world.

In 2011, uprisings in the Arab world gave rise to a classic display of the domino effect. One country after the other experienced massive riots that led to the overthrow of longstanding governments. The riots spread from one country to the next as though they were connected by some invisible wires.

Tunisians removed their longstanding president Zine El Abidine Ben Ali who had ruled from 1987 to 2011.

Then Egypt's longstanding President Mubarak who had ruled from 1981 to 2011 was ousted after Tunisian style riots.

The revolts continued in Oman, Bahrain, Yemen and Libya.

These are classic examples of the domino effect on nearby countries.

CHAPTER 6

How the Seeds of Instability Are Sown by Those Who Leave You

Be not deceived; God is not mocked: for whatsoever a man soweth, that shall he also reap.

Galatians 6:7

Every time someone leaves in rebellion he sows a seed towards his own future. Perhaps, this is the most important reason why you should grow in loyalty and faithfulness. Disloyalty is a seed that you would not want to reap from. In this chapter, I want to share about the seeds that a rebellious person plants towards his future. These seeds will grow and come back in a stronger and larger way.

If you are not spiritual, you will not believe in the power of Galatians 6:7, "Whatsoever a man soweth he shall reap." Many things we see happening today are the results of seeds that were sown yesterday.

Many ministers struggling with division, disloyalty and confusion have sown those seeds in their ministry. These things have grown up and come back to haunt them. Fasting and prayer cannot remove a tree that you planted. Binding and loosing cannot prevent the laws of God concerning sowing and reaping. If you do not want to reap certain harvests you must learn not to sow certain seeds.

This message is for people who have sown certain seeds and want to uproot them. This message also serves to warn you not to sow certain seeds whose fruits you cannot live with. Please believe the Word of God that is spoken to you today. Whatsoever a man sows he will reap!

He Broke One of My Pillars, He Lost Two Pillars

Some years ago, I had a pillar on which I depended. He was my associate pastor and I did everything in the ministry through him. He did announcements, he led the worship and he stabilized the congregation whilst I travelled.

One day a minister of the Gospel enticed him to leave my side. This was a very difficult experience because my entire ministry depended on this pillar. I was heartbroken and suicidal when this happened to me. A few months later, I visited a senior man of God who made a comment that stuck in my heart. He said, "If you break somebody's house to build your house your house will also be broken.

How true that is! Do you expect people to stand by silently as you build your house with blocks from their broken house?

A few years later, I watched in disbelief as the ministry that had taken my pillar began to disintegrate. They had looked so strong at the time they took my pillar. That ministry originally had one senior pastor and two pillars. To my amazement, that senior pastor lost his two pillars within a year.

You see, he took one of my pillars but he lost two. You must be careful what seeds you sow because you will have to reap them one day.

Jeroboam and Absalom provide the best examples of people who sowed the seeds of rebellion and reaped a harvest of instability and continued rebellion. In the text which I have reproduced below, you will see how Jeroboam and Absalom reaped a painful harvest from the seeds they sowed.

1. Those who leave you sow seeds that deprive them of authority.

Those who leave you sow seeds of disloyalty and rebellion.

Jeroboam left the kingdom of Israel, taking with him ten of the tribes of Israel. This departure in itself was a seed of uncertainty. Jeroboam then sowed the seeds that led to his eventual destruction. He established altars in Dan and Bethel, creating alternative places of worship for the people of God. Then he created feasts which God had not asked him to and ordained priests from the most unlikely group of people. All these actions were the seeds that led to his eventual destruction.

Jeroboam Sows the Seeds of Instability

And Jeroboam said in his heart, now shall the kingdom return to the house of David:

If this people go up to do sacrifice in the house of the Lord at Jerusalem, then shall the heart of this people turn again unto their lord, even unto Rehoboam king of Judah, and they shall kill me, and go again to Rehoboam king of Judah.

Whereupon THE KING took counsel, and MADE TWO CALVES OF GOLD, and said unto them, It is too much for you to go up to Jerusalem: behold thy gods, O Israel, which brought thee up out of the land of Egypt.

And HE SET THE ONE IN BETHEL, and THE OTHER put he IN DAN. And this thing became a sin: for the people went to worship before the one, even unto Dan.

And HE MADE AN HOUSE OF HIGH PLACES, and MADE PRIESTS of the lowest of the people, which were NOT OF THE SONS OF LEVI.

And Jeroboam ORDAINED A FEAST IN THE EIGHTH MONTH, on the fifteenth day of the month, like unto the feast that is in Judah, and he OFFERED UPON THE ALTAR. So did he in Bethel, sacrificing unto the calves that he had made: and he placed in Bethel the priests of the high places which he had made.

So he offered upon the altar which he had made in Bethel the fifteenth day of the eighth month, even in the month which he had devised of his own heart; and ORDAINED A FEAST UNTO THE CHILDREN OF ISRAEL: and he offered upon the altar, and burnt incense.

1 Kings 12:26-33

2. **Those who leave you reap a harvest of uncontrollable people.**

Those who leave you reap a harvest of instability.

Jeroboam reaped a harvest: his kingdom was unstable. He was unable to reign for more than two years. A few years later a rebellion successfully overthrew Jeroboam's son. Jeroboam reaped a harvest of uncontrollable people. He realised that he could not control the people. He knew that the people he had led against Rehoboam would rebel against him and kill him if they got the chance.

> And Jeroboam said in his heart, now shall the kingdom return to the house of David: If this people go up to do sacrifice in the house of the Lord at Jerusalem, then shall THE HEART OF THIS PEOPLE TURN AGAIN UNTO THEIR LORD, even unto Rehoboam king of Judah, and THEY SHALL KILL ME, AND GO AGAIN TO REHOBOAM king of Judah.
>
> 1 Kings 12:26-27

How to Destabilize Your Family

There was a pastor who was sent on a mission to establish a church in an Asian country. As he was doing the work, he ran into various difficulties and became depressive and rebellious towards the authorities that had sent him. He began to communicate poorly until he stopped communicating altogether. Eventually, he rebelled openly and left the church without giving any reasons whatsoever.

His wife was not in favour of his actions as she saw the rebellious elements in his speech and attitude. She tried to convince her husband to change his mind about the things he was saying and doing but he would have none of it. He stomped off suddenly and rudely, severing all ties with his former pastor and other people he had known for many years.

Everyone must be careful about the seeds he sows. A few years after his departure, he equally began to lose control over his own family. His wife suddenly decided to leave him. She had become uncontrollable and had decided to abandon the family without any further discussion.

This pastor was beside himself, wondering what he could do to prevent his family from breaking up.

When I heard about it I thought of how ironical it was. This man's wife was leaving him suddenly and without reason. That is exactly what he had done to his pastor and his home church a few years before.

When you practice rebellion and disloyalty, it returns to you in a greater measure. This brother had sown the seeds against his own authority. He was now deprived of the authority he needed to govern his own family!

Perhaps the most terrible rebel a minister can have is a rebellious wife. She is the rebel you are instructed to love. If the demonic spirit of rebellion can get into a wife she becomes the most deadly tool to be used against the man of God. On different occasions I have seen wives of ministers completely filled with the spirit of rebellion by which they tried to control their husband and destroy their ministries.

Who Will Be Destroyed?

On one occasion, the wife of a minister was determined to leave her husband publicly. She wanted the whole world to know that she could not live with him. This minister was deeply concerned about this because he knew that the reputation of his ministry depended on his being happily married. His wife also knew that but she did not care. Many people, including her own mother, begged her not to leave her husband. Eventually, this lady's mother died and all restraint was gone. She threw her husband's things out of the house and publicly separated from him.

The spirit of rebellion seeks to destroy everything that has been built. This lady, bless her heart, would listen to no one. She made the divorce public so that the man would be seen for what she thought he was. Indeed the divorce had a devastating effect on the man of God. Several of the pastors he had brought up and a section of his congregation obviously deserted him.

But it was not only *his* life that was destabilized. That is the point I am trying to make. The instability that you sow into somebody's life is equally reaped by you. Her life became equally unstable as she moved around like a branch cast forth from a tree.

Mutiny on the Bounty

I once watched an enlightening film called "The Bounty". This story highlights the point that you deprive yourself of future authority when you sow certain seeds. It was a film about the true story of a British expedition in 1787 to the Pacific Island of Tahiti to gather breadfruit pods for transplantation in the Caribbean as slave fodder.

The Bounty sailed west to round the tip of South America but failed due to harsh weather and had to take the longer eastern route. Finally arriving in Tahiti in October 1788, Captain Bligh found that due to the delays the wind was against him for a quick return journey, so he decided to stay on the island for four months longer than originally planned. During that time, ship discipline became problematic and many of the crew developed a taste for the easy pleasures that island life afforded.

It is then that the mutiny led by a gentleman called Christian takes place. Playing on Christian's obvious resentment against Captain Bligh's treatment of both him and the men, the more militant members of the crew finally persuade Christian to take control of the ship.

Bligh is roused from his bed and arrested, along with those considered loyal to him and all of them are forced into the ship's launch, minimally supplied and cast adrift.

Blissfully happy at their newfound freedom (though Christian feels remorse and understands the implication of what's been done) they naively sail back to Tahiti to collect their wives, girlfriends and native friends.

King Tynah of Tahiti is shocked by this turn of events. He makes them aware that, as mutineers, their presence on the island could incite King George to declare war against Tahiti and against his people. Realising the folly of staying, though some did, they gathered supplies and sailed away to find a safe refuge.

The search for a safe haven was long and seemingly impossible as they realised that any pursuing Royal Navy vessels would search all known islands and coastlands to find them.

By this point, those that remained on board The Bounty are so frustrated that they are ready to rebel against Christian, the leader of the mutiny, in order to turn the ship back towards Tahiti. After Christian forced the crew to continue on, they eventually found Pitcairn Island; a place which Christian realised may not be marked on British maps on the region and therefore provided their best hope of avoiding the royal navy.

Captain Bligh, through excellent seamanship successfully managed to reach civilization after a very harrowing journey. The crew of The Bounty then burnt their ship to keep it from being found.

Can You Lead These People?

One of the things that struck me as I watched the mutiny on the film, The Bounty, were the parting words of the legitimate captain to the rebel leader. As the captain entered the little boat to which he was being escorted, he turned and asked Christian, the rebel leader, ***"Can you lead these people?"***

This is the big question all mutineers must be asked. This is the key question all conspirators and rebels must ask themselves, **"Can you lead these people?"** Can you lead people you have inspired into rebellion against a rightful leader? The answer is "No, you cannot."

The people you are leading will never be loyal to you. They have learnt how to rebel and to overthrow legitimate authorities and they will surely practise it when they get the chance. Indeed, that is what happened. Christian, the rebel leader, was unable to control the other mutineers.

Can a pastor govern a group of rebellious church members he has led away from their legitimate leader? The pastor must be asked the same question: *"Can you lead these people?"*

The answer is "No, you will not be able to lead them. You will not be able to silence their rebellious way of speaking. You will not be able to quench the continuous murmurings and grumblings that come from them.

You will not be able to prevent the hatred and conspiracies around you. You will never have the stability you desire.

Why? Because you have sown the seeds of instability and rebellion. You have taught your followers how to rebel and dislodge legitimate leaders. They have learnt it well and they learnt it all from you! You are their greatest inspiration for disloyalty. The seeds of instability and disloyalty have been sown and the harvest must be reaped!

3. Those who leave you sow seeds of conspiracy.

Absalom left his father and sowed the seeds of conspiracy and treachery. He planned and plotted against his own father. He overthrew his father with his own father's subjects.

> Absalom said moreover, Oh that I were made judge in the land, that every man which hath any suit or cause might come unto me, and I would do him justice!
>
> And it was so, that when any man came nigh to him to do him obeisance, he put forth his hand, and took him, and kissed him.

> And on this manner did Absalom to all Israel that came to the king for judgment: so ABSALOM STOLE THE HEARTS OF THE MEN OF ISRAEL.
>
> 2 Samuel 15:4-6

4. Those who leave you reap a harvest of treachery.

Some people cannot understand why they continually have rebellious and treacherous people around them. Perhaps, they should consider the seeds they have sown in the past. Absalom was the classic conspirator and he received the full harvest of the same treatment. He was brought down by his own treacherous medicine. Someone in his own camp lied and pretended until he was totally destroyed. Absalom reaped a painful harvest of treacherous behaviour from Hushai the Archite. Read it for yourself:

> Now someone told David, saying, "Ahithophel is among the conspirators with Absalom." And David said, "O Lord, I pray, make the counsel of Ahithophel foolishness."
>
> It happened as David was coming to the summit, where God was worshiped, that behold, Hushai the Archite met him with his coat torn and dust on his head.
>
> David said to him, "If you pass over with me, then you will be a burden to me.
>
> But if you RETURN TO THE CITY, AND SAY TO ABSALOM, 'I WILL BE YOUR SERVANT, O king; as I have been your father's servant in time past, so I will now be your servant,' then you can thwart the counsel of Ahithophel for me.
>
> Are not Zadok and Abiathar the priests with you there? So it shall be that whatever you hear from the king's house, you shall report to Zadok and Abiathar the priests.
>
> Behold their two sons are with them there, Ahimaaz, Zadok's son and Jonathan, Abiathar's son; and by them you shall send me everything that you hear."

SO HUSHAI, David's friend, CAME INTO THE CITY, and Absalom came into Jerusalem.

2 Samuel 15:31-37 (NASB)

Then Absalom and all the people, the men of Israel, entered Jerusalem, and Ahithophel with him.
Now it came about when Hushai the Archite, David's friend, came to Absalom, that Hushai said to Absalom, "Long live the king! Long live the king!"

Absalom said to Hushai, "Is this your loyalty to your friend? Why did you not go with your friend?"

Then HUSHAI SAID TO ABSALOM, "No! For whom the Lord, this people, and all the men of Israel have chosen, his I will be, and with him I will remain.

Besides, whom should I serve? Should I not serve in the presence of his son? AS I HAVE SERVED IN YOUR FATHER'S PRESENCE, SO I WILL BE IN YOUR PRESENCE."

2 Samuel 16:15-19

CHAPTER 7

The Seeds of Stability

David's kingdom was stable to the very end. He had more authority as an old dying king lying in bed, than many heads of state have today. Pastors need to have that kind of authority in their churches. A single instruction from the pastor should be able to instil loyalty and quell uprisings within the ranks.

Why was David's throne so stable? The throne of David was stable because he sowed the seeds that give a person authority.

Unstable churches

An unstable church is one in which there are constant uprisings and rebellions. The Bible speaks of a king against whom there is no uprising.

… and a king, against whom there is no rising up.
Proverbs 30:31

Unstable churches have the unfortunate problem of having leaders, associates and assistants constantly rising up against the leader. There are often a lot of breakaways in the church. There may even be church splits.

Within the congregation you often find groups that have different opinions about different things. Within the congregation, there is often a lot of murmuring and grumbling about many trivial things. Many times the roots of the instability come from the beginnings of the church. Many leaders sow the seeds of instability, disloyalty and treachery at a point in their ministry.

Whenever I see unstable churches I often ask myself, "What seeds has this person sown?" What spiritual roots are growing deep within the foundation of this ministry?

I Sowed a Bad Seed and Quickly Uprooted It

Many years ago, I broke away with the branch of a ministry I belonged to. At the time I did not think there was anything wrong with what I had done. I felt they were not in step with what the Spirit was doing and I needed to march on with the Holy Ghost. I was sure that I was right and they were wrong.

One day however, the Lord showed me in a vision the picture of a broken down ministry that needed a great restoration. To cut a long story short, the Holy Spirit convicted me that I had made the mistake in the way that I had gone about starting the ministry. *He made it clear to me that I was wrong and they were right.* I found myself now in great difficulty not knowing how to correct what I had done.

The Lord asked me to apologise to them and ask them what to do. I was received mercifully and forgiven for my sins. I am always grateful for the graciousness of the leadership of that ministry. Through the mercies of the Lord, I was able to uproot the seed of rebellion that I had planted towards my own future instability.

Dear friend, what seeds have you sown for your ministry? If you are a spiritual person you must believe in the spiritual principles of the Word; whatsoever a man soweth he shall reap.

The Stable Throne of David

The throne of David is the picture of God-given authority. David stands for God-given authority as Solomon stands for God-given wisdom. Remember that only three kings were able to maintain authority over the tribes of Israel: Saul, David and Solomon. No one else had the authority to rule over all Israel. The throne of David was so stable that Jesus' throne will be established in the throne of David.

> **For unto us a child is born, unto us a son is given: and the government shall be upon his shoulder: and his name shall be called Wonderful, Counsellor, The mighty God, The everlasting Father, The Prince of Peace.**
>
> **Of the increase of *his* government and peace *there shall* be no end, upon THE THRONE OF DAVID, and upon his kingdom, to order it, and to establish it with judgment and with justice from henceforth even for ever. The zeal of the LORD of hosts will perform this.**
>
> **Isaiah 9:6-7**

The Seven Seeds of Stability

1. Sow a seed of stability by allowing God to put you into your position without touching the Lord's anointed.

Do not manipulate anything. David allowed God to make him the king.

> But David said to Abishai, "Do not destroy him, for who can stretch out his hand against the Lord's anointed and be without guilt?"
>
> David also said, "As the Lord lives, surely the Lord will strike him, or his day will come that he dies, or he will go down into battle and perish.

> The Lord forbid that I should stretch out my hand against the Lord's anointed; but now please take the spear that is at his head and the jug of water, and let us go.
>
> 1 Samuel 26:9-11 (NASB)

2. Sow a seed of stability by not rebelling against legitimate authorities.

David did not rebel against the legitimate anointed king. Saul committed many sins which could have been a basis for rebellion. David did not rebel against Saul. He just ran away.

> Now it came about on the next day that an evil spirit from God came mightily upon Saul, and he raved in the midst of the house, while David was playing the harp with his hand, as usual; and a spear was in Saul's hand.
>
> Saul hurled the spear for he thought, "I will pin David to the wall." BUT DAVID ESCAPED FROM HIS PRESENCE twice.
>
> 1 Samuel 18:10-11 (NASB)

3. Sow a seed of stability by being good to the fathers.

It is not your place to rebuke or correct fathers. "Correction upwards is rebellion." David did not rebuke his father Saul. Instead he was good to him.

> And it came to pass, when David had made an end of speaking these words unto Saul, that Saul said, Is this thy voice, my son David? And Saul lifted up his voice, and wept.
>
> And he said to David, Thou art more righteous than I: FOR THOU HAST REWARDED ME GOOD, whereas I have rewarded thee evil.
>
> And thou hast shewed this day how that thou hast dealt well with me: forasmuch as when the LORD had delivered me into thine hand, thou killedst me not.

For if a man find his enemy, will he let him go well away? wherefore the LORD reward thee good for that thou hast done unto me this day."

1 Samuel 24:16-19

4. Sow a seed of stability by not eliminating or humiliating your predecessors.

David did not kill Saul when he had the opportunity to. This is an important principle in sowing a seed for a stable ministry. Most young ministers will have the opportunity to humiliate older battle-weary and scarred ministers. That is the point at which you sow a seed towards your future stability.

Then Saul took three thousand chosen men from all Israel and went to seek David and his men in front of the Rocks of the Wild Goats.

He came to the sheepfolds on the way, where there was a cave; and Saul went in to relieve himself. Now David and his men were sitting in the inner recesses of the cave.

The men of David said to him, "Behold, this is the day of which the Lord said to you, 'Behold; I am about to give your enemy into your hand, and you shall do to him as it seems good to you'." Then David arose and cut off the edge of Saul's robe secretly.

It came about afterward that David's conscience bothered him because he had cut off the edge of Saul's robe.

So he said to his men, "Far be it from me because of the Lord that I should do this thing to my lord, the Lord's anointed, to stretch out my hand against him, since he is the Lord's anointed."

1 Samuel 24:2-6 (NASB)

5. Sow a seed of stability by not allowing people around you to fight or eliminate fathers.

David persuaded his men with these words and did not allow them to rise up against Saul. And Saul arose, left the cave, and went on his way.

1 Samuel 24:7 (NASB)

It is equally important to prevent your subordinates and associates from having a rebellious attitude towards authority figures. It is easy to hide behind them and say you have nothing to do with their attacks.

The Spiritual Father, the Spiritual Son and the Spiritual Servants

There was a spiritual son who was constantly in conflict with his spiritual father. He tried to maintain an appearance of a good relationship with his father but it was easy to see the tension and uneasiness that existed between them.

One day, the spiritual father visited his spiritual son in his house. He welcomed him into the living room and entertained his spiritual father, pretending to appreciate the visit. Finally, at the end of the visit, the spiritual father decided to pray for the spiritual son. He prayed powerfully, blessing the spiritual son and his family. Then he left the house and was seen off by the spiritual son.

As soon as the spiritual father left, three young men emerged from one of the rooms in the house. These three young men were spiritual servants of the spiritual son. They had been hiding behind the door listening to the interaction between the spiritual father and the spiritual son.

The three spiritual servants now took brooms and began to sweep the living room prophetically to counter the prayers of the spiritual father. They declared that the prayers of the spiritual father were more of a curse to their master and so they were cleansing the house of this curse.

But the spiritual son did not do anything to stop these three spiritual servants from sweeping away the prayers of the spiritual father. In so doing, the spiritual son lent his approval to the sweeping of these three spiritual servants.

In the future, the spiritual son should expect these spiritual servants to have a disrespectful and rebellious attitude towards authority. The spiritual son should also expect to have lots of trouble from these spiritual servants because he allowed them to rise up against a spiritual father.

On the other hand, King David did not allow his servants to attack King Saul. He did not just abstain himself but he prevented those around him from attacking spiritual authorities. Is it any wonder that he had a stable throne?

6. Sow a seed of stability by moving very gradually into positions of authority.

David moved up gradually from being a shepherd (1 Samuel 17:14-15) to an anointed court musician (1 Samuel 16:23) to becoming a warrior.

David then became a leader of a group of outcasts (1 Samuel 22:1-2). He then graduated to become the king of Judah and finally he became the king of all Israel.

7. Sow a seed of stability by waiting for as many years as it takes to become a man of authority.

Authority is not given to novices. Authority is not given to "men of knowledge without experience". Authority is given to men whose knowledge is tempered with experience and God's love.

David was thirty years old when he became king, and he reigned forty years.

2 Samuel 5:4 (NASB)

CHAPTER 8

The Tragedies of Those Who Leave

A tragedy is an event that causes great suffering, destruction and distress. One of the greatest tragedies I have observed is the tragedy of people destroying their lives by leaving what they should never have left. Much pain and suffering is released when one person moves out of his position.

Perhaps, the greatest tragedy is the waste of life and ministry that is caused by people leaving something or someone God intended for them to stay with. "Leavers" often waste their money, their lives, their giftings and their callings.

Years after leaving, these rebellious people live in isolation, fruitlessness and emptiness. They never became what they were called to be. They never bore the fruit they could have borne by being faithful and staying where they belonged. Unfortunately, many of these "leavers" are in rebellion and never actually repent. Often they do not relate their problems to the fact that they should never have left.

Jesus told the story of two sons who had different outcomes in spite of the fact that they had the same father. This could also be the story of two ministers from the same spiritual father. They illustrate the different outcomes that follow people who go on different paths.

> **... A certain man had two sons: And the younger of them ... took his journey into a far country, and there wasted his substance with riotous living. And when he had spent all, there arose a mighty famine in that land; and he began to be in want.**
>
> **Luke 15:11-14**

1. THE TRAGEDY OF A LOST POSITION.

> **... Father, I ... am no more worthy to be called thy son: make me as one of thy hired servants.**
>
> **Luke 15:18, 19**

If God has not called you to be on your own, do not make the mistake of moving out on your own. If you make this mistake, you will be forced to re-apply for a lower position. Most high positions belong to people who have stayed faithful for many years. Satan's dream is to bring you down. The urge to leave your God-given position is a demonic desire that comes from demon spirits seeking your downfall and disgrace.

As I write this book, I can think of so many people who exemplify this point. Their lives today are a phantom of what they would have been if they had only stayed in their positions.

The Famous Worship Leader

One day, I put on the television and saw a famous Christian singer whom I had not seen or heard of for many years. He had produced several praise and worship albums which contained classic songs that had been sung and are still sang in our churches. Because I recognised this singer, I decided to listen to the interview. To my amazement, I discovered that this singer had fallen prey to the error of leaving his God-given position.

The singer described how he had become one of the most prominent worship leaders of all time. At the height of his fame in the ministry, he had decided to leave his position. He had received invitations from a rich country offering him glorious jobs in other churches.

This famous singer narrated how he had believed those offers and left his position as the most senior worship leader of this very large church and followed the offers of greater glory. He narrated a pathetic story of how he had lost everything he owned.

He explained that when he got to this rich country the offers for employment did not work out as he thought. Most of the promises he had received did not materialise. He was forced to leave the new ministry and launch out on his own. He continued his narration, explaining how his ministry had descended into the darkest hole of his life. He had tried one thing after another with little success.

He confessed on television that he had made one of the greatest mistakes of his life in leaving that church where he was the number one worship leader. He described how he had experienced the loss of ministry, the loss of visibility and a lack of all things, including the lack of a basic job. This man had tried to be the "head of an ant" when he would have been better off as the "leg of an elephant."

I then understood where this minister had been all those years. Just like the prodigal son, he was feeding with pigs whilst he could have been enjoying life at his father's table. What a tragedy it is to leave your God-given position and to follow illusions!

One day I preached in the church where this man had been a worship leader. As I sat on the front row getting ready to preach, I stared at the lady leading the worship and couldn't help remembering the once-famous worship leader. His position had now been filled with people who did not have half of his gifting. What a waste of talent. What a waste of a God-given position.

What can cause a fruitful and successful minister to become a hustling, struggling rebel? The answer is simple. Moving out of your God-given position and wasting the opportunities that would have come to you because of your position. Do you want to follow this example? Certainly not! Decide not to waste the position that you have.

2. THE TRAGEDY OF DESOLATION AND POVERTY.

> **And he said unto him, Son, thou art ever with me, and all that I have is thine. It was meet that we should make merry, and be glad: for this thy brother was dead, and is alive again; and was lost, and is found.**
>
> **Luke 15:31-32**

The father explained to the older brother, "All that I have is for you. I am only having this party to celebrate the return of your brother. In reality he has nothing and you have everything."

Did you say nothing? Is it true that the returning son had nothing? Yes, nothing means nothing. Having nothing is one of the tragedies of leaving your God-given position.

From Grace to Grass

Years ago, I witnessed the rise of a mega church in Asia. This mega church was pastored primarily by a senior pastor and his two associates. This team became a well-known and prosperous team of Gospel preachers. Everyone listened to their messages and everyone looked up to them. However, the day came when one of them decided to leave the team.

One day, this pastor (who was also a pharmacist) was interviewed on television and asked about his vision for his new ministry. He explained how he had single-handedly pastored a church which had grown to over one thousand members. He clearly seemed to have the ability to make it on his own.

This "leaver" felt he was at least as capable as his senior pastor in growing the church (I'm as good as you are).

When I heard that he had grown a church to over a thousand members in such a short period, I was myself impressed and thought that he could probably grow a church. Little did I know that this gentleman had no abilities to handle a church on his own.

After many years, I learnt that he had attempted to start seven different churches and each of them had been a whopping failure.

"What a tragedy", I thought to myself.

This gentleman had been a prominent and flourishing minister. But he had been brought down to nothing by moving out of his God-given position.

The financial difficulties of this failed minister became more and more apparent. This once-affluent and successful minister now tried many different avenues of ministry.

He decided to try his fortunes in different countries. Sometimes I would hear of him in Australia and other times I would hear of him in Latin America. He was offered a good position in a prestigious church but after a while it was clear that he was incapable of holding down a job. After hurling accusations at his employer, he left to try something new.

Then he decided to become a motivational speaker. But no one wanted to listen to him and no one wanted to buy his tapes. He began to be in debt, unable to pay for the production of the CDs of his motivational speeches. He had no money and he had no source of income. Because his pharmacist license had expired, he was unable to get a job as a pharmacist. As his financial crises deepened, old friends of his would give him hand-outs to keep him going.

As I followed this incredible downslide of this minister I could only reminisce of his former glory. It remains to me the starkest example of the tragedy of desolation that follows people who leave their God-given position. Just like the prodigal son, this fellow had "begun to be in want and no man gave unto him."

3. THE TRAGEDY OF WASTED RELATIONSHIPS.

When you leave your God-given position, you lift up barriers between you and your spiritual father. This alters your relationship and cuts you off from the advice and inputs that you could have once received.

By leaving, the prodigal son wasted years of relationship and advice that he could have benefited from. Perhaps this is the greatest tragedy of all; to have access to great wisdom, great fellowship, great anointing and to lose it all because you move out of your position.

4. THE TRAGEDY OF A LOST INHERITANCE.

Elijah had a servant who left the ministry and missed the anointing (1 Kings 18:41-44). This was the servant who assisted him in the slaying of the prophets of Baal. This was the servant who was sent seven times to see if the rain clouds had gathered.

This was the servant who saw the miracle power in the ministry of Elijah. Yet he left Elijah in the midst of his ministry!

When you leave your God-given position, you may lose the anointing you would have received.

When you leave your position, you can also lose your inheritance.

The concept of spiritual inheritance is real. The book of Ephesians teaches us that spiritual inheritance is a reality. "The eyes of your understanding being enlightened; that ye may know what is the hope of his calling, and what the riches of the glory of his inheritance in the saints" (Ephesians 1:18).

If you are a son to your pastor, an inheritance of anointing and spiritual gifts will naturally pass to you - just as property naturally passes from a father to a son. You must receive all the anointing and gifts you can. Don't lose your spiritual inheritance!

Although Elisha had a biological father called Shaphat, he received Elijah as his father and called him "Father". "And Elisha saw it, and he cried, My father, my father..." (2 Kings 2:12). The anointing naturally passed from Elijah to his spiritual son, Elisha.

Have you noticed that pastors who leave their spiritual fathers in rebellion never carry a certain kind of anointing? There are many people who never see a drop of spiritual inheritance because of the way they left home.

When your father is writing his will, how will he know whether you are alive or not? Why should he include you when he has not seen you for so many years? Should he leave his property to a ghost? Certainly not!

CHAPTER 9

How to Identify Those Who Will Leave You

These be they who separate themselves...

Jude 1:19

The Scripture is clear about those who will separate themselves. Those who separate themselves are those who will leave you.

Jude prophesies about these people and devotes his entire epistle to describing people who leave the congregation and separate themselves. With Jude's epistle you can arm yourself with an accurate description of the kind of person who is likely to leave you abruptly.

Please take note of these descriptions because they are useful in helping you to protect yourself from being a victim of defectors.

I predict that the following people will separate themselves:

1. MEN WHO WALK IN THE ERROR OF BALAAM WILL SEPARATE THEMSELVES.

> **Woe to them! For they have gone the way of Cain, and for pay they have rushed headlong into THE ERROR OF BALAAM, and perished in the rebellion of Korah.**
>
> **Jude 11, NASB**

Balaam is famous for charging for his prophecies. The error of Balaam is the error of ministering the Gospel for money. I wish it were not so but many of us are doing the ministry for money.

Pastors of poor churches rarely separate themselves. However, pastors of financially strong churches are often the culprits of the "leaving" syndrome. They need to separate themselves in order to gain control of the power and the money. They do all sorts of things to destroy the church they have hitherto belonged to whilst the Holy Spirit is named as the person who directed them to leave.

Watch out for men who walk in the error of Balaam. Watch out for men who charge for playing the organ, the drums and the guitars. Watch out for people who charge for coming to choir rehearsals. Watch out for people who have to be given "transport money" for every little move they make. Most people who separate themselves walk in the error of Balaam!

2. HIDDEN REEFS WILL SEPARATE THEMSELVES.

THESE ARE THE MEN WHO ARE HIDDEN REEFS in your love feasts when they feast with you without fear, caring for themselves; clouds without water, carried along by winds; autumn trees without fruit, doubly dead, uprooted; wild waves of the sea, casting up their own shame like foam; wandering stars, for whom the black darkness has been reserved forever.

Jude 12-13, NASB

A reef is a ridge of jagged rock, coral, or sand just above or below the surface of the sea. A reef is therefore a source of great danger to ships. Hidden reefs can end the life of a ship suddenly. Men who will leave you are described as hidden reefs. Such men are often hidden from your sight.

This is why it is important to learn about the signs of disloyalty. Many people display these signs before they actually turn on you.

I once watched a film on the life of the famous warrior Chaka Zulu. As I watched him growing up I immediately spotted the signs of a rebellious person. His hatred for his father because of the way his mother was treated was the first bad sign I noticed. But there were several others. His attitude towards his commander in the army, his independence, his stubbornness and his vengeful spirit were all signs of a bloody future.

These people are not so difficult to spot if you know the signs. Both Hitler and Stalin were members of the choir in their churches. Both of them were expelled from school because of stubbornness and rebelliousness.

Stalin was even expelled from a Bible school in which his mother had enrolled him. Both of them were filled with hatred for the existing authorities and challenged them when they had the chance. Indeed, Stalin and Hitler were hidden reefs of destruction waiting for the opportune time to manifest.

Watch out for hidden reefs. Learn to spot them, even in films. Learn how they speak. Understand their language and their posturing. Watch their attitude and you will become an expert in detecting hidden reefs that separate themselves!

3. MEN WHO CARE FOR THEMSELVES WILL LEAVE YOU.

These are the men who are hidden reefs in your love feasts when they feast with you without fear, CARING FOR THEMSELVES; clouds without water, carried along by winds; autumn trees without fruit, doubly dead, uprooted; wild waves of the sea, casting up their own shame like foam; wandering stars, for whom the black darkness has been reserved forever.

Jude 12-13, NASB

People who just care for themselves are dangerous men. A good minister must care for the flock. A good minister must care for others and not just himself. Some people only care when *their* church is being broken. They do not care if *other* churches are being broken. The mass murderers who litter the history of mankind must have not been thinking about others. Hitler's henchmen would murder thousands of people during the day and go home to play with their wives and little children in the evening.

Obviously, they cared about their own families but did not think much about the families they were destroying through their cruelty. Perhaps they never thought of what kind of pain they were inflicting on the world.

Watch out for men who just care for themselves and do not feel sorry for others. A true minister must have a compassionate heart and feel sorry about other people's pitiful situations.

4. CLOUDS WITHOUT WATER AND TREES WITHOUT FRUIT WILL SEPARATE THEMSELVES.

> **These are the men who are hidden reefs in your love feasts when they feast with you without fear, caring for themselves; CLOUDS WITHOUT WATER, carried along by winds; autumn trees without fruit, doubly dead, uprooted; wild waves of the sea, casting up their own shame like foam; wandering stars, for whom the black darkness has been reserved forever.**
>
> **Jude 12-13, NASB**

A close look at rebellious people will reveal that they are clouds without water or trees without fruit. Both of these phrases describe men of straw. Clouds usually bring rain to parched land. The land expects a downpour of fresh water from gathering clouds. What a disappointment when there is nothing in the clouds! What a disappointment when there is no fruit on the tree!

A cloud without water speaks of something without substance. Many rebellious people have no depth. They do not know God nor do they truly fear Him. Anyone who fears God will fear to touch the servants of God. Anyone who really knows God will be afraid to destroy His church.

The church is the bride of Christ and only spiritual people recognize its significance. Only people who love God revere His church and handle it with care.

The proof that a cloud has no water is in its failure to produce rain. You will notice that many of these angry, rebellious "leavers" breathe anger and curses but cannot produce any rain.

They are trees without fruit. The years go by and they disappear into obscurity, bearing little or no fruit. *Years of ministry with little result, is the greatest evidence that people are "clouds without water" and "trees without fruit".*

Watch people who leave churches in rebellion. Carefully monitor their future and you will find out that you were dealing with clouds that had no water!

5. MEN WHO ARE CARRIED ALONG BY WINDS WILL SEPARATE THEMSELVES.

These are the men who are hidden reefs in your love feasts when they feast with you without fear, caring for themselves; clouds without water, CARRIED ALONG BY WINDS; autumn trees without fruit, doubly dead, uprooted; wild waves of the sea, casting up their own shame like foam; wandering stars, for whom the black darkness has been reserved forever.

Jude 12-13, NASB

Men who are carried along by winds are not true leaders. They follow trends and get their strength from the masses. A true leader does not get his strength from the masses! He knows what is right and is not carried along by what the people say. A rebel depends on the support he gets from immature and ignorant people.

I once had an assistant who loved to be in the good books of the people. I soon came to recognize that he really wanted to please everybody. He loved popular opinion and when popular opinion turned against me he followed the popular opinion.

At that time, most of the members in my little church felt I was not called to the ministry. They could not see much future in what I was doing. The church was also filled with a lot of young immature people. The wind of popular opinion blew against me and my assistant was blown along by that wind. This attitude led to his destruction and soon he was no longer found in the ministry.

Watch out for people who are carried along by the winds of the day!

6. MEN WHO ARE UPROOTED, WANDERING STARS WILL SEPARATE THEMSELVES.

These are the men who are hidden reefs in your love feasts when they feast with you without fear, caring for themselves; clouds without water, carried along by winds; autumn trees without fruit, doubly dead, UPROOTED; wild waves of the sea, casting up their own shame like foam; WANDERING STARS, for whom the black darkness has been reserved forever.

Jude 12-13, NASB

Another important characteristic of rebellious people is that they are "uprooted". Every tree is planted somewhere. It is dangerous to be uprooted from where you have been planted. When you meet ministers who cannot tell you where they were trained, you are dealing with men who have been uprooted. These men have become wandering stars because they are uprooted from their true home.

Why do you want to dissociate from the hand that raised you up? Why can't you confidently tell your people about your spiritual father? Why can't you confidently tell others about your spiritual home? It is because you are uprooted and do not properly belong anywhere anymore.

The Spiritual Giant and the Spiritual Son

There was once a man of God who lived in Asia and was very popular and acclaimed in the ministry. This man of God had been raised up by a spiritual giant. This spiritual giant had led him to Christ, ordained him into the ministry and even helped him build his church. The spiritual giant had helped the spiritual son through a recent divorce. These acts alone made this man of God, a son to the spiritual giant. The spiritual giant had gone even further and promoted his spiritual son, making him into one of the most popular ministers of his day in his country.

Unfortunately, this good relationship between the spiritual giant and the spiritual son did not last for long. For various reasons their relationship soured until it was virtually non-existent.

One day, the spiritual son attended the conference of another great international minister and continued to visit these conferences every year. After a while, the spiritual son decided to take this new international minister as his father. It seemed that God had given him a new and blessed relationship. He was a newborn spiritual son to this international minister.

However, even though this spiritual son celebrated his new relationship, he had in reality just been uprooted. To be uprooted means to be disconnected from your original place of planting. Being uprooted is not a good thing! It is a bad sign and it is a biblical description of people who separate themselves.

Many ministers are disconnected from those who raised them up. These separated sons cite many reasons for their separation such as: the sins, the unrighteousness and the downfall of their spiritual mentors. But none of these reasons are good enough to turn yourself into an uprooted tree!

When you are uprooted, you become a wandering star going from place to place hoping to be recognized. It is time to go back home and be planted where you belong.

7. GRUMBLERS AND FAULT-FINDING MEN WILL SEPARATE THEMSELVES.

These are GRUMBLERS, FINDING FAULT, following after their own lusts; they speak arrogantly, flattering people for the sake of gaining an advantage.

Jude 16, NASB

Chronically discontent people grumble and find fault with everything. This is the surest sign that you are dealing with a rebellious person. I once sent several missionaries to different countries. Some of them were successful and others returned home without finishing their mission.

One day, as I mused on the different missions and on the missionaries who had had to return home I realized a common thread that ran through their experiences. Those who returned unsuccessfully were all "brought home" by their wives. Through the bad and *unhelpful attitude* of their wives, they had been forced to give up their missions and return home.

Most of the missionaries did not want to return home but had no choice. At heart, these missionary wives were rebellious against the ministry. They manifested their rebelliousness by *private grumbling* at home. They found fault with their husbands, with the missions and with the countries they were sent to. Of course the wives denied any wrongdoing. However, we knew that their wives were grumbling discontented women.

The fruit of their private hidden grumbling and faultfinding was clear. Every single husband was forced to leave his call and go home. Grumbling is always a bad sign and leads to people leaving their God-given positions.

8. MEN WHO SPEAK ARROGANTLY WILL SEPARATE THEMSELVES.

> **These are grumblers, finding fault, following after their own lusts; THEY SPEAK ARROGANTLY, flattering people for the sake of gaining an advantage.**
>
> **Jude 16, NASB**

Men who speak arrogantly will leave you as Jude prophesied. Watch out for people who have no regard for whom they are speaking to.

You Are Not Always Right

People who speak proudly are dangerous people. One day, I was having a discussion with a young minister. The discussion turned into an argument as I emphasized my point to him.

Finally when he run out of arguments and had nothing to counteract what I was saying, he rebuked me saying, "You are not always right you know?"

I was taken aback.

I was being made to understand that although I seemed to be winning the argument it did not mean I was right.

Although what he was saying was true in essence and although I am not always right, there was a prideful manner in which he was rebuking the person who had appointed him as a pastor and ordained him into the ministry.

Watch out for people who speak arrogantly to men of authority! They are fulfilling the prophecies of Jude. They are men who will eventually separate themselves.

I'm Not Surprised You've Come

One day I visited a junior pastor who had resigned from the ministry. I wanted to reconcile with him and repair our relationship. But I was taken aback at his reception. Instead of being glad that I had come to reconcile and repair the broken relationship, he began to speak harshly to me.

He said, "I'm not surprised that you've come.

He continued, "I was wondering how long it would take you to come.

I couldn't believe what I was hearing because I thought he would be glad to see me. After all I was his pastor and I was the one who had appointed him as a pastor.

As our conversation continued I said to him, "Listen... I…"

Before I could continue he stopped me in my tracks and said, "Don't say *listen*. Don't come here on your own terms."

He continued, "Don't say 'we' it's you, Dag." (He used to call me "Pastor" but when people are angry and rebellious they do not use your titles anymore. They call you by your first name to bring you to their level).

Sometimes rebellious people hate you so much that they cannot mention your name when speaking to others about you. At such times they refer to you as "the guy", "your brother", "that man", "the man" or "your man" depending on which is appropriate to them).

I continued to try to talk to this former pastor but he was so angry. Then he dropped a shocker. He said, "I have survived without you! I don't need you anymore." We all need each other. But he didn't want to talk to me anymore. He got up and ushered me out of his house.

Men who speak arrogantly will leave you as Jude prophesied.

Watch out for people who have no regard for whom they are speaking to! Watch out for people who can say anything to anyone!

9. FLATTERERS WILL SEPARATE THEMSELVES.

> **These are grumblers, finding fault, following after their own lusts; they speak arrogantly, FLATTERING PEOPLE FOR THE SAKE OF GAINING AN ADVANTAGE.**
>
> **Jude 16, NASB**

People who flatter you cannot be trusted. It is the simple-minded who are impressed by the flattery of wicked men. Throughout the Bible we are warned to be careful of flatterers. "For *there is* no faithfulness in their mouth; their inward part is very wickedness; their throat is an open sepulchre; they flatter with their tongue" (Psalms 5:9).

Be on guard every time you meet someone who excessively praises you and your ministry. No one knows who is really pleasing God. No one knows whom God is really happy with. Heaven will reveal it all. Every person I have met who is full of effusive praises has eventually left the ministry. Flattery is a sign of disloyalty. It is a sign of someone who will eventually leave you. His praises are a mask for his true intentions.

I once met a journalist who told me I should be the president of Ghana. He praised me for my achievements saying that they were the greatest proof that I could be the president of Ghana. I asked him why he had not suggested that his own pastor be the president since his pastor had achieved more than I had. He quickly dismissed my remarks saying that his own pastor was of the old stock and was not relevant anymore. I immediately recognized the hallmarks of a dangerous flatterer.

Was that not the voice of Satan trying take me out of my ministry and into foolishness? You must indeed be careful of people who flatter. It is nice when people praise you but remember that a flatterer is a dangerous person!

He that speaketh flattery to his friends, even the eyes of his children shall fail.

Job 17:5

10. PEOPLE WHO CAUSE DIVISIONS WILL SEPARATE THEMSELVES.

These are THE ONES WHO CAUSE DIVISIONS, worldly-minded, devoid of the spirit.

Jude 19, NASB

There are people who are divisive by nature. These people see things through what I call "political" eyes. They see everyone through the eye of nationality, tribe or colour. Such people analyse what you do and make comments according their own political and divisive perceptions.

If you speak to a Nigerian, they would say, "Ei, I see that you like Nigerians very much." If you make a truthful observation about Americans they would say, "Ei, I see that you don't like Americans."

If you are friendly to a light-skinned lady they would say, "Ei, I see that you like fair ladies."

If the boss asks Joe to do a job they would say privately to other employees, "Ei, the boss really likes Joe."

If their father buys a present for his daughter, Adriana, they would say, "Ei, Daddy's favourite child is Adriana."

Meanwhile when presents were bought for them they did not come to those same conclusions.

These people are divisive and see everything as a product of favouritism or unfair power play. They look upon people as belonging to this group or that. Such people will quickly identify how many members of a particular tribe or country are gathered in a room. Such people quickly become conscious of a person's tribe or nationality when it has not occurred to those who are less political or divisive.

Watch out for people who have a divisive eye!

11. WORLDLY PEOPLE, DEVOID OF THE SPIRIT WILL SEPARATE THEMSELVES.

These are the ones who cause divisions, WORLDLY-MINDED, devoid of the spirit.

Jude 19, NASB

It is a very worldly practice to categorise people according to their tribe or nationality. People without the Holy Spirit cause divisions and act like men of the world. A soul is a soul and is precious to God. When God touches your heart, you will love all men. You will not see them as Ghanaian, Nigerian, Zimbabwean or American.

Worldly people have always used human divisions to start wars and to create conflicts.

National Pride, the Reason to Break Away

I once had a West African pastor who wanted to break away and separate himself. Being a worldly man devoid of the Spirit, he began to speak to the congregation about my nationality. He told the other West Africans in the church that I was a Ghanaian and that Lighthouse Chapel International was a Ghanaian church.

He urged the people from his country to sit up and "do something for themselves".

It was in his interest to get the people to think in a certain way and to give them a good reason to follow him. He told the other West Africans that I was only interested in building churches in Ghana.

Meanwhile, our mission to his country was one of the largest and most expensive we had ever undertaken. We had spent so much money, time and effort there, trying to minister the Gospel of Jesus Christ.

But the divisive, worldly minister who is devoid of the spirit will look for things to divide us. Surely, they shall reap the fruits of their works.

12. MOCKERS WILL SEPARATE THEMSELVES.

> **But you, beloved, ought to remember the words that were spoken beforehand by the apostles of our Lord Jesus Christ, that they were saying to you, "In the last time there will be MOCKERS, following after their own ungodly lusts." These are the ones who cause divisions, worldly- minded, devoid of the spirit.**
>
> **Jude 17-19, NASB**

Watch out for people who mock you. Most ministries start out small. Small things are often despised. Young developing ministries are often despised. The shortcomings found in mature ministries can also be mocked at. Instead of mocking, we need to have a tender sympathetic eye for the difficulties people experience. Mockers are dangerous people and they are often disloyal.

One day, I was in a meeting with a group of pastors. They were discussing some breaking news about a senior man of God. The breaking news was that this man of God's wife had decided to divorce him. Everyone was chipping in his opinion about the situation. Some felt that the man of God was an evil man and deserved to have this bad experience. Others were more sympathetic.

In the middle of this discussion, one of the ministers who claimed to be a son to the man of God got up to serve himself some food. He made a disparaging remark about this unfortunate man of God that brought out peals of laughter from the other pastors in the room.

I felt uncomfortable and sad about the atmosphere in the room. I wondered how a son could mock at his father. Surely, this fellow could not be a loyal person.

Do you think a loyal son will mock at his father in his day of his difficulty? This is why the Bible teaches that you should not walk with mockers. "Blessed is the man that walketh not in the counsel of the ungodly, nor standeth in the way of sinners, nor sitteth in the seat of the scornful" (Psalm 1:1).

13. MEN WHO FOLLOW UNGODLY LUSTS WILL SEPARATE THEMSELVES.

> **That they were saying to you, "In the last time there will be mockers, following after their own ungodly lusts." These are THE ONES WHO CAUSE DIVISIONS, WORLDLY-MINDED, DEVOID OF THE SPIRIT.**
>
> **Jude 18-19, NASB**

Men who follow ungodly lusts rarely follow the Spirit of God. Most of the evil done in the world is caused by men who follow ungodly lusts. Presidents who follow ungodly lusts for money and power rarely do anything good for their countries.

Similarly, pastors who do not follow the Lord but rather follow their own lusts rarely do well in the ministry. The lust for power and the lust for money can turn faithful people into devils. Most rebellious people are filled with the lust for power and the lust for money.

CHAPTER 10

How to Fight Wolves

For I know this, that after my departing shall GRIEVOUS WOLVES enter in among you, not sparing the flock.

Acts 20:29

Twelve Things You Must Do to Stabilise Your Ministry

Some people can best be described as wolves. People who break churches and steal sheep are called wolves. The effect they have on the church is the same as a wolf on the flock of sheep. Indeed, there is always confusion after a wolf has raided the flock.

When people leave you, they leave behind a very bad taste, which is difficult to overcome. Honestly, the feeling is similar to the feeling that comes when someone close to you dies.

The church is not spared from the bad feelings and the bad atmosphere that goes with people leaving. Indeed, most "leavers" turn and "pollute the doorway" as their last act to the church. What do I mean by "pollute the doorway"? I mean these people venomously speak evil about the church, its leadership and its pastors. They release poisonous stories and suggestions about everything they have been a part of for many years. They sow the seeds of discontentment in the hearts of people they leave behind. They want everyone who stays behind to feel silly for staying. They want those who remain behind to see the need to also leave.

It is important that you rise up and fight this feeling in the church. If you do not, the domino effect and the polluting effect of the "departee's" evil spirit will devastate your ministry. In this chapter I want to suggest some steps that you need to take to deal with the scourge of "church breakers".

God has called us to build His church and we must learn how to fight wolves. People who break churches and steal sheep are called wolves. A good pastor must have weapons to fight wolves and medicine to poison them.

> **Let the lying lips be put to silence; which speak grievous things proudly and contemptuously against the righteous.**
>
> **Psalm 31:18**

1. IDENTIFY SYMPATHISERS OF THE "DEPARTEE" AND SEND THEM AWAY.

There are always people who are sympathetic to the "departee". Even though they do not leave with him, they sympathise with his cause and feel that he had a point in doing what he did. These people will always be a source of instability.

You must accept that there are people who will never believe in you.

No amount of talking or meeting with them will change anything. It may be difficult to send people away but it is often wisdom to send away the people who cannot be made to believe in you.

Abraham sent Ishmael and all the brothers of Isaac away from Isaac. He knew that they would never support Isaac. He knew that Ishmael who was thirteen years older than Isaac would never submit to the leadership of Isaac.

> **And Abraham gave all that he had unto Isaac. But unto the sons of the concubines, which Abraham had, ABRAHAM gave gifts, and SENT THEM AWAY FROM ISAAC HIS SON, while he yet lived, eastward, unto the east country.**
>
> **Genesis 25:5-6**

Many times separation is the only way to instil stability and harmony after someone has polluted the church with his venom. When a snake bites, it releases venom that poisons the whole body. Even though the point of contact may be the leg, the venom spreads and affects other parts of the body. That is what it is like when a treacherous person has worked in your congregation. Although he may have worked on some people, *many others* are affected indirectly.

Abraham also knew that he would never have peace until Lot left him. There are certain people that have to leave before peace will return. *Confusion will not go away until certain individuals have left your congregation.*

Prayer will not cause stability and peace to return!

Abraham was wise and he knew that the only way for peace to come was separation from Lot.

And Abram said unto Lot, Let there be no strife, I pray thee, between me and thee, and between my herdmen and thy herdmen; for we be brethren.

Is not the whole land before thee? SEPARATE THYSELF, I PRAY THEE, FROM ME: if thou wilt take the left hand, then I will go to the right; or if thou depart to the right hand, then I will go to the left.

Genesis 13:8-9

2. LAY A GOOD FOUNDATION AS TIME GOES BY.

Laying up in store for themselves A GOOD FOUNDATION AGAINST THE TIME TO COME, that they may lay hold on eternal life.

1 Timothy 6:19

The passage of time usually heals hurts and wounds. You must allow for time to pass so that you can fully recover from the experience of someone leaving your ministry. You must recover from the confusion and division.

You must lay a good foundation for the future of your ministry. If you do not use times of peace properly, the problems will re-occur.

In the light of your experiences with "leavers" you must lay a good foundation for the future stability of your congregation.

This good foundation will consist of cleansing, teaching, preparing and growing wiser and more careful.

3. CLEANSE THE CONGREGATION THROUGH TEACHING.

Sanctify them by the truth: thy word is truth.

John 17:17

You need to cleanse the people left behind with the Word of God. You will need to cleanse their minds of the pollution caused by the people who leave. People who leave sow seeds of confusion and uncertainty. But the Word of God has the power to cleanse their minds.

> **Now ye are CLEAN THROUGH THE WORD which I have spoken unto you.**
>
> **John 15:3**

4. FIGHT CONFUSION WITH THE WORD OF GOD.

> **For where envying and strife is, there is confusion and every evil work.**
>
> **James 3:16**

One of the hallmarks of a wolf attack is confusion. Confusion is a situation of panic in which there is a breakdown of order. Confusion is the state of being bewildered or unclear in one's mind about something.

Confusion Is Caused by Lingering Accusations

One day, a close associate of mine decided to break away and start his own church. It was a surprise to us because no one had done anything like that before. After he left, there was confusion in my camp.

Even though I had had issues with him, I had not publicly said anything negative about him before. No one knew that there were questions and problems with this person. He was now saying lots of negative things and stirring up questions and confusion in the minds of the people.

I suddenly realized that I was surrounded by people who were not sure whether I was a good person or a bad person. Was I an evil man posing as a pastor? Were the dastardly accusations and rumours about me true? I could see through the eyes of the people around me. I knew they were not sure anymore.

It took more than a year before the confusion of that attack left us.

Indeed, God is not the author of confusion and I had to battle my way out of the confused and bewildered atmosphere caused by this "departee" pastor.

Notice how John Mark brought confusion between Apostle Paul and Barnabas. Paul and Barnabas were good friends until John Mark deserted Paul in the heat of the ministry. The perfect unity and harmony between Paul and Barnabas was shattered by the actions of John Mark. "After some days Paul said to Barnabas, "Let us return and visit the brethren in every city in which we proclaimed the word of the Lord, and see how they are." Barnabas wanted to take John, called Mark, along with them also. But Paul kept insisting that they should not take him along who had deserted them in Pamphylia and had not gone with them to the work. And there occurred such a sharp disagreement that they separated from one another, and Barnabas took Mark with him and sailed away to Cyprus" (Acts 15:36-39, NASB). Many people who "leave" release the spirit of confusion. I can tell you that God is not the author of that confusion. God is not the one who brings confusion to your church! It is the devil who brings confusion into your ministry through treacherous people.

You can help people overcome their confusion by washing away the uncertainty with the Word of God. Paul taught the Corinthians the truth and that helped them to overcome their confusion. "For God is not the author of confusion, but of peace, as in all churches of the saints" (1 Corinthians 14:33).

As you teach the people the Word of God, confusion will evaporate. You need to know how to teach about loyalty and disloyalty if you are to dispel confusion in your church.

5. CLEANSE YOURSELF OF EVIL SEEDS.

Whether you like it or not, the event of someone leaving has an effect on your spirit. Leavers pollute your spirit with the seeds of hurt, anger, hatred, wickedness and revenge. You will need to pray long and hard to get free from these dangerous spiritual seeds. If you don't cleanse yourself you will fall into the trap of bitterness and unforgiveness.

> **Keep me from the jaws of the trap which they have set for me, and FROM THE SNARES OF THOSE WHO DO INIQUITY. Let the wicked fall into their own nets, while I pass by safely.**
>
> **Psalms 141:9-10 (NASB)**

6. IMPROVE YOUR LEADERSHIP STRATEGIES.

Often your style of leadership contributes to people leaving you. Sometimes though, in spite of the most perfect leadership strategies, people still stir up strife against you. There is nothing you can do about it.

King David said there were elements who stirred up hatred, strife and war against him even though he just wanted to dwell quietly in the land. Likewise there are people who stir up division and conflict even though all you desire is to peacefully serve the Lord.

> **Let not them that are mine enemies wrongfully rejoice over me: neither let them wink with the eye that hate me without a cause. For they speak not peace: but THEY DEVISE DECEITFUL MATTERS AGAINST THEM THAT ARE QUIET IN THE LAND.**
>
> **Psalms 35:19-20**

It is important that you work on yourself to ensure that your leadership methods are not causing instability in your church. You must analyse yourself, search yourself and seek for wisdom lest you have brought division and church splits through your own foolishness.

When you have re-established yourself with the good counsel of the Word you will be ready for the next phase of your ministry.

"Every purpose is established by counsel: and WITH GOOD ADVICE MAKE WAR" (Proverbs 20:18).

7. FORGIVE DISLOYAL PEOPLE.

And when ye stand praying, forgive, if ye have ought against any: that your Father also which is in heaven may forgive you your trespasses.

Mark 11: 25

As a minister you desperately need your prayers to be answered. You cannot afford to retain the seed of unforgiveness that prevents your prayers from being answered. There is only one thing that God will not forgive you for and that is when you do not forgive others. A minister of the Gospel seriously, critically and desperately needs to have his prayers answered. He cannot afford to retain the negative seeds within his heart.

Therefore I say unto you, What things soever ye desire, when ye pray, believe that ye receive them, and ye shall have them. And when ye stand praying, forgive, if ye have ought against any: that your Father also which is in heaven may forgive you your trespasses.

Mark 11:24-25

8. DO NOT LET THE REST OF YOUR MINISTRY BE COLOURED BY MISTRUST.

People who leave you can make you mistrust those who stay with you. People who leave cause great damage because they destroy your life's work. Sometimes they take away your stability, your livelihood and even your health. It is not easy to be loving and trusting after bad experiences. After experiences with breakaways, you may simply not trust people anymore. But this is yet another trick of Satan – to make you suspicious and untrusting.

A lack of trust will hurt the people who remain with you. A lack of trust reveals continuing bitterness in you. The pollution caused by these characters must end!

You cannot allow the bitterness caused by these experiences to direct your future ministry and prevent your prayers from being answered.

Looking diligently lest any man fail of the grace of God; lest any root of bitterness springing up trouble you, and thereby many be defiled;

Hebrews 12:15

When bitterness and mistrust fill the heart of a minister it discolours his ministry. Decisions are taken based on his bad experiences. When you meet a minister who is bitter, you sense a certain weakness in him as well as a certain deviation from his true calling.

The Untrusting Senior Pastor

Some years ago, I met a senior pastor whom God had called to begin branch churches. He was so excited because he had a new building to relocate to. His plan was to start a second church in a new property that he had acquired. He went ahead with his plans and left the majority of the old congregation with his associate pastor whilst he moved to the new property. He was so excited because he saw this as a way to expand his work and ministry. But it was not to be.

Within a few years of leaving his associate at the old place, the associate stole the hearts of the people and led them to break away from their leader.

This pastor was dumbfounded and completely heartbroken.

He said to me, "I left all the established families and the oldest church members with this associate. If I had known he would break away I would have taken them all with me."

He concluded, "I am not starting any more branches. All I want is to have one church in one location."

I felt sad as I realised that this pastor had decided to give up church expansion because of the bad experience he had had.

In some churches the senior pastor has no trust for anyone and therefore does not appoint anybody else as his assistant. The only other person allowed to preach is the pastor's wife. Obviously this limits the ministry and does not allow other ministers to develop.

I remember another pastor who was vehemently opposed to the idea of having cell groups. He felt they would break away and form splinter churches. His church was one large sea of people with no sub-groups. You can imagine the strain on the pastor and his wife!

People who have encountered disloyalty often come to have variants of their original ministry. You can hardly blame them for reacting defensively to possible repeated attacks by "wolves in pastors' clothing." Whatever your variant of ministry is just make sure it is not influenced by bitterness.

9. DO NOT CURSE RANDOMLY.

> **And he loved cursing; so let it come unto him. And he delighted not in blessing; and let it be far from him. And he clothed himself with cursing like his vestment; so let it come into his bowels like water, and like oil into his bones; Let it be unto him as a garment with which he covereth himself, and for a girdle wherewith he is constantly girded.**
> **Let this be the reward of mine adversaries from Jehovah, and of them that speak evil against my soul.**
> **Psalms 109:17-20 (Darby Bible)**

You must be careful of issuing random curses on people who hurt you. You must realise that you sometimes also hurt others without knowing what you are doing. None of us would like to be cursed for the mistakes we have made. Paul said, "Bless them which persecute you: bless, and curse not." (Romans 12:14).

Some of the people who turn against you do so out of immaturity. God in His mercy will give them an opportunity to grow and mature. Every child is rebellious at a point, but it is the father's duty to accommodate this rebelliousness until the child returns to his senses. "But when he came to his senses, he said, 'How many of my father's hired men have more than enough bread, but I am dying here with hunger!" (Luke 15:17, NASB).

10. USE CURSES TO PROTECT YOUR CONGREGATION.

There are times the Holy Spirit directs you to speak a curse.

The First Curse

Many years ago, I was preaching on a topic I called "The New Wave Churches". Getting to the end of the sermon I found myself speaking prophetically. I began to issue curses on people that would destroy the churches. The curses were directed at those who would destroy the churches that were being planted.

I was not conscious of the fact that I was proclaiming curses but as I looked back and remembered the things I had said, I realised that the Holy Spirit had led me to issue curses against wolves, sheep scatterers, sheep thieves, splitters of congregations and destabilizers of churches. This was a form of spiritual protection for the new wave churches that I was planting.

As the years went by, I realised that those pronouncements were a constant protection for the churches the Lord was using me to establish.

The Second Curse

One day I was on a flight from Ukraine to another city in Europe. I was on my way to visit one of our churches. I did not know what to do because there had been a lot of confusion in the church I was going to visit.

This confusion had been caused by people who had left and poisoned the rest of the congregation.

Suddenly the Holy Spirit told me, "When you get there, place a curse for the protection of the church."

I was quite surprised by this instruction, but the Lord told me, "When you lead a congregation and do not have the power to physically protect them, you must place spiritual barriers to protect the sheep. There are certain things you cannot physically prevent wolves from doing. But you can issue a spiritual perimeter curse that will serve as a barrier for the wolves."

I want to give you two scriptural examples of this.

Paul's Curse

The apostle Paul in dealing with the Galatians did not know who or what was bewitching the group he had laboured for. The church he had laboured so hard to build was being destroyed by false doctrines and other pollutions. As he stood by helplessly, and unable to do anything but write a letter, he spoke a curse against anyone that would bring a new and false doctrine to the congregation.

> **But though we, or an angel from heaven, preach any other gospel unto you than that which we have preached unto you, let him be accursed. As we said before, so say I now again, If any man preach any other gospel unto you than that ye have received, let him be accursed.**
>
> **Galatians 1:8-9**

John's Curse

On another occasion, John the revelator wrote to the churches describing in detail the end-time apocalypse as well as giving important messages to the church. As he finished writing this epochal letter, he realised how people could change what he had written or modify what he had written to suit their purposes. Unable to control the future and unable to control human beings with their varied motives, he issued a blighting curse on anyone who would modify his writings.

> **For I testify unto every man that heareth the words of the prophecy of this book, If any man shall add unto**

these things, God shall add unto him the plagues that are written in this book:

And if any man shall take away from the words of the book of this prophecy, God shall take away his part out of the book of life, and out of the holy city, and from the things which are written in this book.

Revelation 22:18-19

You will see from these two examples that curses must be deployed by spiritual leaders when they have no other way to protect the congregation. Whether you like it or not, both blessings and curses are issued by holy men of God.

11. OVERCOME YOUR FEAR OF REBELS.

One of the things that goes through your heart when people leave is the fear of failure. Is everybody leaving? Will others leave? Is this the end? Will my ministry come crashing down? You cannot help but have these thoughts.

The pastor's ministry depends on the gathering of people. The departing of people is the exact opposite of what he is trying to achieve. The leaving of people is the nullification of all the pastor's work. The departure of one or two people sometimes has a cascading effect and leads to many others leaving as well.

Many a pastor has heard horror stories in which a five-thousand member church was reduced to a two hundred member church. Many pastors have heard of how large congregations were divided in two by strong and charismatic assistants who had the goodwill of the congregation.

This is what we fear. We fear that one-day everything will come crashing down and we will be left in a hall with no one. But you must overcome this fear because fear is an evil spirit. The dangerous thing about fear is that it guides you when the Holy Spirit should guide you.

When you are filled with fear you do not react properly to the pollutions created by "departees." You will not rise up with strength and stabilize your congregation as you should. You will be timid about things you should not be timid about.

Accusations have a weakening effect because there is always some truth in every accusation. But you must be strong and bind the spirit of fear. The righteous are as bold as a lion. You must be bold and strong when dealing with rebels.

Rebellious people will leave you with nothing if you allow them. You must fight them fearlessly. You must not allow confusion to weaken your hand. Strike them out and fight them with everything you've got. "Flash forth lightning and scatter them; Send out Your arrows and confuse them.

Stretch forth Your hand from on high; Rescue me and deliver me out of great waters, Out of the hand of aliens whose mouths speak deceit, And whose right hand is a right hand of falsehood.

I will sing a new song to You, O God; upon a harp of ten strings I will sing praises to You, Who gives salvation to kings, Who rescues David His servant from the evil sword.

Rescue me and deliver me out of the hand of aliens, Whose mouth speaks deceit And whose right hand is a right hand of falsehood" (Psalms 144:6-11, NASB)

After that take up your microphone and preach powerfully about love and Christ. Do not think you are an evil man because you have had to deal with such people. You must "Let the high praises of God be in your mouth, and a twoedged sword in your hand" (Psalms 149:6.). You must learn to combine fighting and worshipping.

Have you never watched lions in their natural habitat?

Do you see how brutal they are?

Do you see what killers they are?

Do you see how they love blood?

Yet do you see how loving they are with their cubs?

Do you see how they play with their young and live together as a family?

Our Lord is the lion of the tribe of Judah. He will destroy His enemies but He will love His sheep. Come on and be like David. Be a brutal fighter and a loving shepherd!

Listen to his prayers against the enemies of righteousness:

"Let not them that are mine enemies wrongfully rejoice over me: neither let them wink with the eye that hate me without a cause. For they speak not peace: but they devise deceitful matters against *them that* are quiet in the land. Yea, they opened their mouth wide against me, *and* said, Aha, aha, our eye hath seen *it*. This thou hast seen, O LORD: keep not silence: O Lord, be not far from me. Stir up thyself, and awake to my judgment, even unto my cause, my God and my Lord. Judge me, O LORD my God, according to thy righteousness; and let them not rejoice over me. Let them not say in their hearts, Ah, so would we have it: let them not say, We have swallowed him up. Let them be ashamed and brought to confusion together that rejoice at mine hurt: let them be clothed with shame and dishonour that magnify themselves against me" (Psalm 35:19-26).

12. BUILD NEW RELATIONSHIPS TO REPLACE BROKEN ONES.

One of the sad things that happen when people leave in the wrong way is the breaking up of good relationships. Unfortunately there are going to be relationships you cannot maintain if you want to follow the will of God.

You must move on and form new relationships with new people that God brings into your life. I can assure you that there is a replacement for everyone that walks away from you.

No one is indispensable and you will learn this even if you don't believe it to be true. Sometimes there are over two hundred people waiting to replace people who do not value their position and walk away from it. God is doing a new thing. Open your heart and receive a new day with new relationships. Accept that God can use other people in your life.

Years ago I had a worship leader whom I was used to. He was a charming pastor and a nice worship leader. I was used to having him as my right-hand man. One day, to my surprise, he decided to turn against me. When he eventually left, I wondered who or how his position would be filled.

But God raised up others to do his job. I would never have known those other people if this fellow hadn't moved away. Sometimes the departure of a person heralds the arrival of God's choice for you.

It was when Saul's heart departed from following the Lord that the man after God's heart was revealed. We would never have known about David if Saul hadn't been unfaithful to the Lord.

In everything give thanks. God is going to raise up the Davids of your ministry who will live and die for you in faithfulness and loyalty.

CHAPTER 11

The Response That Those Who Leave with Our Children Should Expect

A pastor once said to me, "You have one thousand churches. Why don't you allow me to take one?"

Another pastor said, "You have so many members; why are you over-reacting because I have just taken a few of them with me?"

I find these questions preposterous, to say the least.

What kind of response would you expect if you came to visit me in my house and took one of my children away with you when you were leaving?

Would you expect me to agree for you to take one of my children away with you because I have four children? Would you be bold enough to say, "You have four children so just allow me to take one of them?"

I may have four children but each one of them is precious to me. I would not allow anyone to visit me and deceive my little daughter to follow him. She obviously would not know what she was doing.

Obviously, this is how absurd it sounds when people leave your ministry with some of your members and say, "O you have thousands of members, just allow us to leave with a few of them."

People who try to leave our churches with our hard-won members must expect certain responses from us. This chapter elucidates the biblical responses a pastor must give to those who leave churches and try to take our members with them.

1. Those who leave and take our children with them should expect THE RESPONSE OF A BEAR ROBBED OF HER WHELPS.

> I WILL ENCOUNTER THEM LIKE A BEAR ROBBED OF HER CUBS, and I will tear open their chests; there I will also devour them like a lioness, as a wild beast would tear them.
>
> Hosea 13:8 (NASB)

Do you expect us to be happy with you for taking away our children?

Do you expect us to accept it quietly? Certainly not!

You must expect us to charge at you and rip open your chest. Expect the response God promised to give to rebellious people through the prophet Hosea. It is the response of a bear that has been robbed of her cubs!

Expect us to attack you to try to get our babies back. Do not think you can walk away with our offspring whom we have laboured so hard for. We will attack you like a bear robbed of her whelps. Do not think we are out of our minds because of our ferocious response to your taking our members with you.

Those who leave with our children and our members should expect that we will be relentless enemies. I suggest that you watch the response of buffalos to the lions who constantly try to steal their young. It is a ferocious death and life struggle. This is the natural response of parents whose young are under threat.

2. Those who leave and take our members with them should expect THE RESPONSE THAT HUMAN BEINGS GIVE TO A KIDNAPPER.

Kidnapping is the taking away or the transportation of a person against his will. The kidnapping of children is called child stealing as this is often done with the intention of keeping the child permanently.

Many rebellious pastors are also spiritual kidnappers because they leave churches with the young and innocent ones. Spiritual kidnappers have the intention of keeping these young ones as their permanent members.

Human beings respond to kidnappers by using the police, the military, and any other forces at their disposal. A pastor who leaves a church and takes away a group of members should expect the same kind of spiritual response. Expect us to follow him with every weapon at our disposal until we retrieve our stolen children.

3. Those who leave and take our members with them should expect THE RESPONSE THAT HUMAN BEINGS GIVE TO A THIEF.

a. Expect us to come out against you with swords and clubs.

> And Jesus answered and said to them, "Have you come out with swords and clubs to arrest Me, as against a robber?"
>
> Mark 14:48 (NASB)

b. Expect to be smitten till you die.

> If a thief be found breaking up, and be smitten that he die, there shall no blood be shed for him.
>
> Exodus 22:2

c. Expect to be made to pay double for what you have taken.

> If a man shall deliver unto his neighbour money or stuff to keep, and it be stolen out of the man's house; if the thief be found, let him pay double.
>
> Exodus 22:7

4. Those who leave and take our members with them should expect THE RESPONSE THAT HUMAN BEINGS GIVE TO A KILLER.

Since the person who takes away our members is a thief he should expect us to act as though we are dealing with a thief. A thief does three things: stealing, killing and destroying. People who steal laptops and mobile phones have been known to kill as well. Jesus Himself said, "The thief cometh not, but for *to steal*, and *to kill*, and *to destroy*: I am come that they might have life, and that they might have it more abundantly" (John 10:10). We will not be happy to relate with the life and ministry of a murderer.

> **Moreover ye shall take no satisfaction for the life of a murderer, which is guilty of death: but he shall be surely put to death.**
>
> **Numbers 35:31**

We will therefore relate with all stealers of church members as though we were relating to killers and murderers. Do not expect us to be friends with those who steal church members. Do not expect us to ordain you. Do not expect us to recommend you. We will relate with you as we would relate to a thief who comes to kill.

5. Those who leave and take our members with them should expect THE RESPONSE THAT HUMAN BEINGS GIVE TO A DESTROYER.

Every person in his right mind must stay away from destroyers. Jesus said a thief comes to steal, to kill and to destroy. Anyone who steals your sheep is also a destroyer. If you steal our sheep or our members, expect us to ostracise you because you are a destroyer! Expect us to do what the Psalmist said.

... I have kept me from the paths of the destroyer.
Psalms 17:4

You must also expect us to rejoice when the destroyer of our country and our church can no longer harm us.s When Samson was rendered powerless by the Philistines they rejoiced gleefully.

> When the people saw him, they praised their god, for they said, "...Our god has given our enemy into our hands, EVEN THE DESTROYER OF OUR COUNTRY, Who has slain many of us."
>
> Judges 16:24 (NASB)

CHAPTER 12

How to Pray about Those Who Cause Trouble When They Leave You

Fifteen Keys to Praying against Disloyal Men

1. Pray that you may be delivered from evil men wearing the cloak of a minister of the gospel.

Deliver me, O Lord, from the evil man: preserve me from the violent man;

Psalm 140:1

2. Pray that you may be delivered from the people around you who are planning things in their hearts.

Deliver me, O Lord, from the evil man: …Which imagine mischiefs in their heart...

Psalm 140:1-2

3. Pray that you may be delivered from the people around you who stir up conflict, controversies and strife.

Deliver me, O Lord, from the evil man: … continually are they gathered together for war.

Psalm 140:1-2

4. Pray that you may be delivered from the criticism of the sharp and serpentine tongues of disloyal people.

Deliver me, O Lord, from the evil man: ...They have sharpened their tongues like a serpent...

Psalm 140:1, 3

5. Pray that you will be delivered from the poison of the accusations of disloyal men.

Deliver me, O Lord, from the evil man: ...adders' poison is under their lips...

Psalm 140:1, 3

6. Pray that you may be delivered from people who want to destabilize your ministry.

Keep me, O Lord, from the hands of the wicked; preserve me from the violent man; who have purposed to overthrow my goings.

Psalm 140:4

7. Pray that you will be delivered from the proud members of your team of leaders.

The proud have hid a snare for me, and cords; they have spread a net by the wayside; they have set gins for me. Selah.

Psalm 140:5

8. Pray that the Lord will protect you and help you as you contend with disloyal and ungrateful people.

O God the Lord, the strength of my salvation, You have covered my head in the day of battle.

Psalm 140:7 (NASB)

9. Pray that God will not allow the plans of wicked people to destabilize your work and ministry.

Grant not, O Lord, the desires of the wicked: further not his wicked device; lest they exalt themselves. Selah.

Psalm 140:8

10. Pray that burning coals of fire will fall on people that speak mischief behind your back.

As for the head of those that compass me about, let the mischief of their own lips cover them.

Let burning coals fall upon them: let them be cast into the fire; into deep pits, that they rise not up again.

Psalm 140:9-10

11. Pray that those that hate you and accuse you to destroy your life will be cast into a fire.

Let burning coals fall upon them: let them be cast into the fire; into deep pits, that they rise not up again.
Psalm 140:10

12. Pray that people around you who speak mischief be thrown into deep pits from which they cannot arise.

Let burning coals fall upon them: let them be cast into the fire; into deep pits, that they rise not up again.
Psalm 140:10

13. Pray that all the slanderers and evil speakers around your life will not have any footing or be established in your congregation or in your team of leaders.

Let not an evil speaker be established in the earth: evil shall hunt the violent man to overthrow him.

Psalm 140:11

14. Pray that evil shall hunt the wicked and the evil man in your midst and that their effect on your life and ministry will be overthrown.

Let not an evil speaker be established in the earth: evil shall hunt the violent man to overthrow him.

Psalm 140:11

15. [77]Pray that your ministry will maintain its focus.

I know that the Lord will maintain the cause of the afflicted, and the right of the poor.

Psalm 140:12